My GOD-GIVEN *Life*

CECILIA DOREEN DETTLER

Copyright © 2024 Cecilia Doreen Dettler.

All rights reserved. No part of this book may be reproduced, stored, or transmitted by any means—whether auditory, graphic, mechanical, or electronic—without written permission of both publisher and author, except in the case of brief excerpts used in critical articles and reviews. Unauthorized reproduction of any part of this work is illegal and is punishable by law.

ISBN: 979-8-89419-121-8 (sc)
ISBN: 979-8-89419-122-5 (hc)
ISBN: 979-8-89419-123-2 (e)

Because of the dynamic nature of the Internet, any web addresses or links contained in this book may have changed since publication and may no longer be valid. The views expressed in this work are solely those of the author and do not necessarily reflect the views of the publisher, and the publisher hereby disclaims any responsibility for them.

THE EWINGS PUBLISHING

One Galleria Blvd., Suite 1900, Metairie, LA 70001
(504) 702-6708

Foreword

A good book has a beginning and end. Sandwiched between these two parts in this book is the story of my humble yet busy life. Appearing on the following pages you will see most of the aspects of my eighty-nine years here on earth. I had two goals for the book. First, my twin sisters are twenty-two years younger than I am. I wanted to show the huge differences that took place in the world including such things as housing costs, food costs, and social interactions in just one generation. My second goal was to show my complete adoration and love for God, Jesus, and the Blessed Virgin Mary. My story here is divided into four main parts. I have used many names of people in these pages. I consider them all wonderful relatives or friends, and I love them all dearly. There are also farms, schools, towns, and geographic places mentioned here that were instrumental in forming the person that I became. God placed all these in my life so I would always have His guidance.

Part 1: 1934 to 1953

In the first part here, I have arranged in chronological order the places I lived in from birth until marriage, life through the early years, and continuing until I graduated from high school. There are some fun childhood stories. You will be introduced to my immediate family. Also appearing will be numerous relatives that played such a wonderful and loving role in my life. Learning of the many physical hardships that were ever present in the years following the Great Depression should provide some education and humor for you!

Part 2: 1953 to 2024

My marriage and my life until today—you will learn of our wonderful family that began in 1953. Much time will be spent on the comings and goings of marriage life that is so different from the modern era. You won't learn so much about the kids' lives as they have their own stories to tell. My marriage was full of personal fulfillment. You will learn why I say this. I was always busy, and time has passed, as it is commonly said, "like the blink of an eye."

Part 3: My God-Given Life

This is the heart of my story. My faith in God is the most important part of my entire being. I have been a servant of the Lord as He guided me through life. I am at the firm belief that the most important goal in our lives is saving your soul for God and attaining heaven for all eternity. You will see firsthand the hardship I faced in my life to keep God in charge every day! There have been incredible satisfying days and mind-numbing disappointments.

Part 4: Who Is Doreen Dettler? Fifty-One Story-Worth Questions

This is a fun part of the book as I answer fifty-one questions about myself. Subjects like favorites, embarrassing moments, business ideas, marriage, children, relatives, and money are discussed! If you haven't grasped "Who Is Cecilia Doreen Dettler" in parts 1, 2, and 3, this will help you to define me!

The following page shows a map of the very Northeast corner on North Dakota. I spent my entire life of Eighty nine years in this small area. Canada is the top of the page. The X"s show where I was born, where Grandma and Grandpa Fritz were located, where Grandma and Grandpa Carignan were located, where we lived when I was younger and went to country school, and finally where we lived after marriage.

Google Maps

Birth place
X
Carignan's

The Fritz's
X
Home/school
X

Home pre marriage
X

Dettler Farm/marriage
X

Part 1

1934 to 1953

It's December 2023, and I've decided to write a few things about my life. Now at age eighty-nine, it is hard to believe I've lived to be this "old." God truly has a plan for everyone, and it appears that mine includes, for now, to live to at least the ninth decade. Two years ago, after a great many prayers, I made the decision to leave my home in Langdon, North Dakota, and become a resident in Osnabrock, North Dakota. I became a resident at the Osnabrock Community Living Center. Some of my children were astonished at my decision.

I simply said, "It's time and the right choice for me." As of this date, it has been the right decision. I absolutely enjoy my time here and have made some wonderful new friends. The staff treats us with so much respect. Three meals and laundry done every day—what more could I ask for?

I was born June 21, 1934, at Leroy, North Dakota. My birth took place at our home, which was very normal during this time in history. Daddy and Mom were living and farming on the Martineau farm southeast of Leroy, thus my birthplace. Grandparents and family members were always an important part of babies being born. I have few details about my birth except that I was the first child born to my mother and father, Edward and Jennie Carignan.

Early picture of Mom and Daddy.

We lived in this farmhouse, and it was our home until 1941. We stayed here until I was in second grade. It was a very cold two-story house with a single stove in the living room on the first floor providing heat. No running water or electricity. This was very common for farmhouses when I was young. My siblings Rita, Ronald, and Melvin were also born in this house. As with my birth, I'm not sure which relatives were there to help with the births, but you can bet someone was there. It was just what people did! Below shown here are the dates for my three siblings born at the Martineau farm. Now it seems strange to think that children were born at home without the use of drugs. Women indeed have a huge tolerance for pain!

Rita—December 13, 1935   **Ronald—October 6, 1937**

Melvin—January 24, 1939

I want to show some other members of my immediate family tree even though I know you can get these from family history books also.

Daddy's parents were **Gideon Carignan and Aurelia Lame**.

Mom's parents were **Theodore Koropatnicki and Mary Cymaseau.**

Here is a list of Mom's and Daddy's brothers and sisters including their spouses:

Carignan

Gideon and Delia

Bill and Tina

Fred and Frieda

August Carignan

Charlie and Alice

Ed and Jennie

Malvina and Ernest Lemier

Eva and Joe Clifford

Blanche and John Kalis

Eleanor and Gene Martineau

Koropatnicki

Jennie and Ed Carignan

Nick and Cecelia

Annie and Harvey Plante

Bill and Myrtle

Mike and Joyce

Pete and Mary

Joe and Marion

Lena and Ozzie Warner

Emilia and Bill Wilkinson

These names will be important as there will be times when I talk of visiting them or have stories to tell about them.

The following is a picture of Mom's parents.

Theodore and Mary Koropatnicki (aka Fritz).

Dad farmed along with his brother Charlie. Uncle Charlie, unmarried at the time, lived with us. As said earlier, we farmed the Martineau farm, which was one of the nicest farms in the area. I'm not sure of the size of the farm nor the arrangement Daddy had with the Martineau family, but it kept us all busy. I remember seeing the threshing equipment and the cook cars that the women used to feed the harvest crew. How those women worked! There were no trees on the farm, so it was hot for everyone.

Pictures at the highly productive Martineau farm in 1940. Left: Mom and Daddy with me, Rita, Ronald, and Melvin. Right: One of the first years without a threshing crew.

The late 1930s and early 1940s was a transition time on farms. Tractors were starting to show up, as the picture above shows, yet horses were still very much part of the workforce. The picture on the next page shows bundles of grain being hauled to the threshing machines. Tractors were expensive, and farms still had pasture and horses, so it took some years to complete the change to mechanized agriculture.

Horses were still being used on farms in 1942.

My mom told me that she and Daddy were married August 6, 1933, with a very nice simple wedding at St. Joseph's Church in Leroy. The reception was a simple dinner at Daddy's mother's (Aurelia Lame Carignan) house in Leroy and no honeymoon. They went back to the farmhouse as it was threshing time (harvest), so Daddy had to be there. They couldn't be alone because, as stated above, Uncle Charlie was there with them at the house. He lived with us until I was about thirteen years old.

One memory of Uncle Charlie was how he was able to kneel on the bare wood floor as Mom and Daddy prayed the Rosary. Grandma Carignan also lived with us during the winter months. Her house was a very small log house, and I don't think it would have been very warm. My best recollection of Grandma Carignan is staying with her in Leroy. We attended mass every day. At the house, I loved the smell of her fragrant petunias. One time I was so lonesome and with no telephones to call home I needed to be cuddled.

We lost Grandma Carignan a little before Christmas. She choked on a piece of meat and had surgery. She never recovered. She had left her small cold home again and had come to live with us for the winter. It seemed so strange without her. I remember the wake service was at her daughter's at Leydon—Aunt Eva and Uncle Joe Clifford's house. As usual, a rosary was prayed. The men always led the Rosary, and it was very customary to say it often including during the day and in the evenings.

Grandma's death caused my first sad feelings of losing a loved one. Elaine, the youngest in the family, came to the wake. I couldn't believe how she cried. She had lived a long way from Grandma, and it showed how she missed her. This scenario really stayed with me. I don't remember the funeral, but she was buried at the Leroy Cemetery.

My mom's father, Grandpa Koropatnicki, or Grandpa Fritz, as we called him, came from Austria to Canada. I don't know much about him as he was a very quiet, kind man. I do know he liked to have a beer or two on Saturday night. Mom's mother, Grandma Fritz, came from Ukraine when she was fifteen years old. She wanted to go to Canada so bad that her parents agreed to sell two cows to cover the expense of the travel. In the meantime, she got cold feet, but her folks said she had to go! She came to Canada and worked as housekeeper for some rich people. Soon she became pregnant with my mother, Jennie. Not much was ever said about this situation as it was certainly out of the normal in this time period to be an unwed mother.

Then she met Grandpa Fritz, and they were married just north of the Canadian border in Caliente, Manitoba. They came to Walhalla, North Dakota, and rented land there to farm. Success allowed them to buy land near Backoo, North Dakota, where most of their nine children were born. This is the place I remember the most. Grandma Fritz was a very hard worker inside and outside the house. My mom was her right hand until she married.

They built a new barn on the farm and had a barn dance when it was finished. It always seemed to me they didn't have much money, but they must have had enough money to pay for the barn. This was really something. We used to stay with them quite often as we lived about ten miles away. I loved the rhubarb with salt and gooseberries. Grandpa and Grandma spoke Ukrainian, so we had a hard time to understand the words. One thing we knew when Grandma got loud with Grandpa, things weren't good. At night, Grandma coughed a lot, and I assume she had allergies.

Ukrainian Christmases were something special and as kids we used to wait for. As there were no telephones, Grandma would send Uncle Bill or Uncle Mike personally to invite us. We were always so thrilled! I loved the perogies, cabbage rolls, and cooked wheat. Don't know when she had time to make all those dishes, which were made for everyone. Then Christmas Eve, we would put on a Christmas program. We sang carols and recited poems we had done at our school Christmas programs. Grandma loved it. Of course, Joe and Emilia were our age and helped us to put on a good show.

Mom would be telling her parents all that was taking place in our family. In those days, there were no Christmas presents, just candy and nuts. It's important to note here a huge difference in habits then and today. I can't imagine a Christmas without presents anymore. Too many presents today, and we could use more focus on Jesus's birth.

For Christmas, a year when I was a teenager, I got a brush and comb set. I displayed it on my dresser over an embroidered dresser scarf Mom had made for me. I loved that then and still like doilies. I have also made many hundreds of doilies over the years. I was upstairs one time before Christmas in a room they weren't using for a bedroom. I saw some packages that showed up at Christmas. That was a big letdown as I then knew the truth about Santa. Christmastime was the one of the rare times when we would have food between meals. We might get a snack after school, but in general, we had our three meals and were always hungry at those times compared to today when it seems that eating goes on all day. Thus, we were not fussy eaters, which made it easier for Mom to cook for us.

Grandpa Fritz developed diabetes and was bedridden for quite a while, and Grandma took care of him. Oh, the beddings she must have washed. She lived on the same farm for most of her adult life. Bill, their son, cash rented the farm after Grandpa's death. She had to move to allow Bill and his family to have the house. Before she left, the gas water heater needed fixing. Her son Pete was in the basement, trying to fix the heater when it blew up. He was burned badly, and Grandma Fritz was blown from the house into the yard. Thank God no one was killed. I'm positive that Grandma would have said her favorite saying at this point, which was "*Bosha me, Bosha me.*" In English, this was "God help me!"

With the house not livable, she moved to a low-rent housing in Walhalla where she lived until almost ninety-one. I loved her a lot, but it seemed I didn't get the honor of being her favorite. In my mind, it seemed that honor went to Rita!

I do not remember that much sickness in the family although it seemed someone always had a cold. One day Daddy got a kidney stone. Mom had to drive him to Gretna, Manitoba, Canada, which was the closest bigger hospital. His pain was so bad, so he was on the floor of the car. This really scared us kids. Don't know what they did, but he survived.

There were no trees on the Martineau farm, so it was hot for everyone. In the winter, the snow piled in the yard. One nice winter day, Mom and Daddy were going to Grafton.

They took us to stay at Grandma's. When they got home and shut the house door, the blizzard of March 1941 hit. Of course, no phones, TV, or radio to warn Grandma and Grandpa Fritz. They wondered how Mom and Dad were. We stayed here for a few days and had a wonderful time with them until the storm ended. Uncle Mike was in the woods when the storm hit. He returned home safely on his horse because by nature, horses can always find their way home—even in a blizzard. God was good to keep everyone safe.

I loved to go to Aunt Eleanor and Uncle Gene's farm. It was a big house, and it even had a pantry. I thought that was pretty special—but not as cool as the toilet that was upstairs. It even flushed by pulling on a long rope. That must have been hooked to a barrel up top, and it worked great. I always remembered the pretty light fixtures too. Mr. Martineau, who owned the house, was wealthy at that time—so different than most.

I started first grade at a country school near Leroy. I didn't mind it at all. Back in the day, the school would have about ten to twelve students representing all twelve grades with one teacher for all these students. She or he had to be very knowledgeable in all subjects, which, as you know, is different than today when teachers specialize in only one grade.

One of my embarrassing moments happened while on the teeter-totter in the school playground. Four of us were on each end, and I'm in the middle. We were having so much fun and laughing that I wet my pants. It ran down to the kids in front of me and to the four people on the other end. I was so embarrassed. I guess I must have stayed outside until my pants dried. Oh dear!

My first-grade teacher took me to Walhalla after school one day. We went to her parents' house, and I thought it was the "Taj Mahal." I had never seen anything as nice as that. Funny the things you remember as a child. Of course, our house had the bare necessities and showed me at an early age the very real differences in people's wealth.

I remember at about this age Mom making Rita and me dresses for Easter. That was quite a treat. Don't remember if we got a new hat or new shoes—I would bet not. I also don't recall any of our clothes being made from flour sacks at this time. We were glad not to be embarrassed because Mom had not used the flour sacks although she did make aprons out of the sacks, which was okay. The first dress I bought on my own with working money was when I was a freshman in high school. Believe me, I wore it a lot. I had ordered it from the Sears catalog. It didn't cost much as I didn't have much. It looked nice too. Thank you, God!

The hard work on the Martineau farm allowed Daddy to buy, in 1941, three quarters of land located six miles north, a quarter mile east, a quarter mile north of Cavalier called the Swanson farm. It wasn't the best land as it had an artesian well that had flowed for years and made some of the land too salty to produce a crop, but at least it was now owned. In order to buy the Swanson farm, Daddy evidently borrowed some money. His being the first time in his life, he was afraid to walk down the street until it was paid back. He was afraid the bank would ask for the money and he wouldn't be able to pay it back. In those days, you didn't buy fertilizer. The manure from the cows, pigs, and horses was used on the fields. Chicken manure was used on the gardens. It all worked well.

The house was big and nice for a two-story farm home. There were hardwood floors, and we even had closets in the bedrooms. Daddy dug a well in the yard, and the water was good. There was also a pig barn and a shop where Daddy and Charlie worked on the equipment. The flies were really bad. I suppose all the animals and chickens were the source. Mom used to hang ribbon tapes from the ceiling, which were sticky. She also put water that contained something in it I didn't know, but it was a real attractant, and the flies would die. Many times she took a dish towel, gave us one, and opened the screen door, and we would all chase them back outside—worked for a short period. Daddy and Charlie also built a grain elevator that I wish I had now as a memento.

Back to the barn—in the winter, we had large snowdrifts between the house and the barn they had to shovel out steps to get over the snowbanks. These were necessary to bring the water and milk to the house. I'm sure this and many other farm chores was the reason I don't recall anyone being overweight back then. There was also a henhouse, and I loved to gather eggs or watch a hen hatch a newborn chick. I was somewhat afraid of the fierce rooster that protected the chickens' home!

There were four bedrooms upstairs, but it was cold. During the winter, there was lots of frost on the windows.

Mom washed clothes on Mondays and usually was still washing as we returned from school. I suppose it took longer because of the time to heat the water. The washer had a gas motor, and the exhaust pipe went from it to the window. Must have kept the room awfully cold with a window open. It also took a long time to get the motor started. The washed clothes were hung on what was called a clothesline. This was a good-sized rope or wire that was hung between two poles. The clothes were then attached to the wire by clothespins. There was no such thing as a clothes dryer on farms. Later in life, bags of clothes were actually hung together, but whites and diapers were always outdoors. Clothes smell so good when dried this way, and we didn't need Bounce or other deodorized products. The bedsheets were the first to appear on the clothesline as they were always washed first.

The house had a summer kitchen, and Mom was so glad to move out there. We had a water cistern, which was a wood-lined hole in the basement used to store water, usually rainwater, so she could pump the water from this to the summer kitchen instead of hauling it. This was a big change for sure.

In this house, we had a gas lanterns for light. Outside of candles, these were our only source of light. They had what were called mantles that were lit with a match, and then they burned the fuel, which was located below in a small tank. I couldn't understand how something so small could give so much light. We also had many kerosine lamps, and they were very smoky. Therefore, the glass shades on the lanterns had to be washed every afternoon. That was a job for the kids. Like most young kids, we did our chores out of love for our parents. That is written with a little satire—although I think we were pretty good with helping out where we could.

A cabinet like Mom had in the kitchen.

The house didn't have many features on the inside that made life easier for Mom, but she did have a well-put-together cabinet. A copy of what she had is pictured on the previous page. She loved it—so handy for sifting flour and other cooking preparations.

Since there weren't any toilets, there was a potty that every day had to be dumped out in the outdoor toilet house. Then they had to be washed and Lysol poured in to make it smell nice. The potty was what we used for nightly bathroom visits. It was always kept in Mom's room, so we had to come downstairs to use it. I don't know how Mom and Daddy slept with all the traffic coming into the bedroom at night to use the potty. Rita and I had to take turns and no missing either. Daddy must have used the barn. I know the older boys had to kneel to use it. Good thing the floor was made of wood or linoleum. We didn't have toothpaste, so at night, we used baking soda to scrub our teeth. I don't know if this was responsible for making my teeth so soft, but I got dentures at a very early age.

At night we would hang our underwear either on the doorknob or close to the stove that was in the living room. It was much warmer here than upstairs, so we had something warm to start the day. We wore only dresses or skirts and long socks, so again nice to start warm underneath. Slacks for women or girls was something we did not know about!

The Swanson house had a big basement also. Mom sure canned a lot. I know we snapped many quarts of beans and podded peas. That was easy as Mom and Dad had to work the garden and take care of picking the vegetables I can't remember ever losing any of the garden produce to a hailstorm. The garden also produced potatoes that required sometime in the spring to take off the sprouts. This was a procedure that allowed the potatoes to remain good until summertime—until the new crop arrived.

As kids we were told to clean our plates. They always told us stories about the starving kids of the world. Not sure how they knew of the starving kids, as there was very little sources of news, but it helped us finish our meals. At the end of the meal, if we finished our plate, we could turn it upside down and get dessert. Now what child wouldn't do that!

I went to second grade at a country school located only about a mile from the farm. It was called Crosby Number One school. No electricity or running water. There was a bucket in the basement of the school that we used to go to the bathroom. It had to be dumped and cleaned every day—Lysol again.

I sometimes went to summer school, and it was so hot. I'd be sick to my stomach on many days. Probably would have helped to drink more water. I really got the two extremes of weather on the farm: cold and hot.

When I was in third grade, I went to a declamation contest in Cavalier from our school. I was to recite a poem up on the high stage, so out I went; and when I saw how far away everyone was, I froze in my tracks and I said my poem, but I was so scared, and my voice was so weak that no one heard me. Obviously, no ribbon!

I was never much for playing tricks on people. One time at Crosby school, when I was maybe in sixth or seventh grade, I took an egg to school. I put it under the teacher's bell. Well, you know what happened when she picked it up to ring it. I don't remember my punishment (in school or home), but I needed it. I have no idea why I did it. It was the only time I did something so ridiculous. I'm not even sure why the thought came to me. Maybe the standard answer applies—"the devil made me do it."

One of the great things in the house was the smell of homemade bread or cinnamon rolls, which Mom had ready when we came home from school. I always liked the crust as it was so good when fresh. We also had what were called dinner boxes. These were thin hinged flat boxes that we used instead of paper bags. I guess these were a precursor to the backpack kids use today. We didn't always have meat sandwiches, but the cheese was so good, and sometimes we had yummy homemade jelly. One thing, we weren't starving. We didn't have much, but we were so happy.

Even though happy, Mom and Dad didn't show much affection. I did see them kiss and sit next to each other on the couch. I thought their love was good. I never witnessed them having a fight—not even one!

As I write this, I have to compare then to today. It seems society, as a whole, has gone to more affectionate gestures. Many more hugs and kisses.

There was only one time I was afraid. Dad and Mom were at the fair and I was babysitting the younger kids and the baby was fussing. I think it was Louis. The thunder and lightning was so bad. I know I was sure relieved when they returned home.

I loved to go to Aunt Elanor and Uncle Gene's farm. It was a big house that even had a pantry which even at the age of ten or eleven I thought was great. They also had a toilet upstairs that you could flush. There was a long rope that you could pull that opened a barrel up top. They didn't have plumbing, so the water may have been stored rainwater. I remember the pretty light fixtures. Mrs. Martineau, who owned the place at the time, was wealthy—so different from most.

A rendition of a horse-drawn sleigh used to gather supplies in town.

We used a team of horses to travel to Bathgate to pick up coal briquets. These were burned in either a stove or what was called a stoker, which augured the coal into a chamber to be burned. We used a coal bucket to haul coal either down to the basement or to haul clinkers to the dump. Clinkers were the by-product after the coal was burned.

Coal was used as it burned hotter and longer than wood. Ice was also picked up in Bathgate at the same time as coal. The ice was used to keep food somewhat cold as there were no electric refrigerators.

As stated earlier, Mom had a big garden. There were also plum trees in the yard, and they were so good. The plums made an excellent tasting jam, one of the family favorites.

The schoolhouse was about one-half mile from the farm. I know you've heard this "walter way back story"—about how we walked to school in the snow and both directions uphill. At least some of that story is acurate. Both ways in the snow was true, but the uphill part both ways was obviously exaggerated.

During the winters, we used horses, and a flat sleigh called a stone boat for rides to and from school. The stone boat was used to haul manure from the cows that were spending their winters inside the barn. Consequently, we used clean straw to sit on as we rode on the more aptly called "the manure boat." To stay warm, we had blankets that were made from horsehair. They were kind of itchy but kept us warm on the ride to and from school.

Daddy ready with the stone boat "alias manure boat," ready to take me to school.

We had a swing in the back that Daddy made for us. Made from an old tire, it was in a tree close to the house. We sure loved it. I remember the weeds got so tall that we had to cut them with a scythe before we could swing. The mosquitoes were everywhere. There were no lawn mowers to help. Also made lots of mud pies, playing house in the toilet (outhouse) with our dolls. So simple were the days and us.

Daddy and Uncle Charlie used some curse words. They were sharply corrected by Mom. One day, as Rita and I were walking from school, she got mad at me. I had no clue as to why, but she swore at me. I don't think I tattled on her, but I never heard her swear again.

Here at the Swanson house, relatives didn't live very far away; so almost every Sunday, we visited them, or they came to visit us. If they came to our house, Mom would go out, catch two chickens with a chicken grabber, cut their heads off, pluck the feathers after they were dipped in a big pot of boiling water, clean them up, and serve them for supper. Today there may be a few people that would think the chickens hadn't been dead long enough.

A bit of an interesting note here—we grew up calling our meal, which would be served in the evening, supper. It seems today many people call this dinner. Our noon meal was called dinner, and today that is lunch. Our lunches were midmorning and midafternoon.

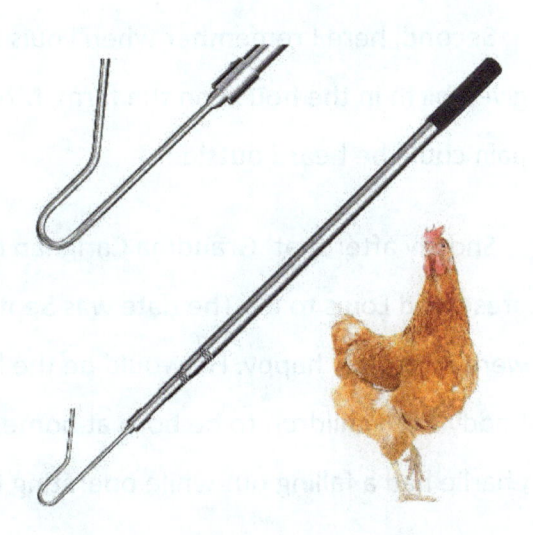

A chicken grabber!

After Sunday mass, there was a store open to get gas or groceries. We usually got a treat of five cents to buy candy of some kind for ourselves. My choice was a box of Luden's cough drops. They were black and licorice tasting, and I loved them.

In the summer of 1947, a tornado flattened the barn with some cattle in it. The entire family was in the basement and were scared the house was going to go. According to Ronald, it rained eleven inches during the storm. After the storm, out in the yard there were chickens without any feathers. Just as unusual was a mother hen sitting on her chicks in the open yard. There was also a six-inch branch that the high winds had stuck into the house siding. The treetops were almost touching the ground.

Second, here I remember when Louis was born. Having given birth in the house on the farm, Mom's groans from the pain could be heard outside.

Shortly after that, Grandma Carignan came outside and presented Louis to us. The date was September 4, 1941. We were incredibly happy. He would be the last of Mom and Daddy's ten children to be born at home. Daddy and Uncle Charlie had a falling out while operating the Swanson farm.

It may have been complicated, enduring two tornadoes on the farm. In 1948, for whatever reason, Daddy and Charlie decided to sell out and go their separate ways. In the spring of 1949, we moved to a house located one mile north and one mile west of Cavalier. This was called the Becker farm.

Update of the family at the Swanson farm, includes Louis.

This house was so cold. It was by far the worst I had been in. Daddy tried to put some kind of material that was used normally on the outside of houses to keep it warmer. He put it on the inside of the house. It was no warmer, but now it was also gray and ugly. It's hard to express the miserable conditions we lived in here on these pages, but we were still happy. Daddy and Mom worked so hard to make the house livable.

The house was very small with a porch, kitchen, one small bedroom, and two small bedrooms upstairs—not much space for a family of eight—and guess what, no running water or electricity. I am about to enter high school and still have not experienced living in a house with modern utilities.

Daddy took a job at a car shop in Cavalier. This probably furthered his quest for car knowledge that stayed with him for the remainder of his life. Speaking of cars, I do remember a funny story here. We took a picture Kodak camera. It was the four kids (myself, Rita, Ronald, and Melvin) plus Mom and Daddy.

The photograph was us surrounding a new car that Daddy had bought. The Kodak company gained knowledge of the picture when they developed the film and wanted to buy it. Looking at the picture now, I'm perplexed as to why it was so important for them. Yes, a great-looking family, but certainly not unusual, but I guess they wanted to do some advertising for their film. Mom made the decision and said, "Absolutely not." It wasn't that it wasn't a good picture, but Mom said, "No one is going to wipe their bottom a—— with our picture." She didn't curse often, but she meant it here. I never heard about the amount of money they offered, but whatever it was, the amount would not move Mom to accept the offer.

Daddy, Mom, me, Rita, Ronald, and Melvin.

Jerry was born while we lived on this farm. Rita and I made aprons to help Mom when she came home with Jerry from the Park River Hospital. The date is September 19, 1949. I remember Mom having him in an oval clothes basket when she brought him in the house. This may seem odd, but I had seen some kid's crib being a dresser drawer. Imagine that today! They might put you in jail for child abuse. I know you are asking, "How in the world did we survive?" With the addition of Jerry, the small house got even smaller.

Since there was no television, radio was a big part of life. They were battery operated. Dad always listened to the news especially in the evenings. During the day, at times he could be found listening to the markets. We knew better than interrupting him while he listened. Mom liked to listen to one lady and her program. She gave out recipes, and Mom loved them. There were very down-to-earth foods. Then she would listen to music too. Daddy was not interested in music, but Mom loved to sing along. Mom and Dad bought a used piano from a lady in Langdon. Mom loved to pick out her songs on it. Too bad she hadn't taken some lessons; I think she would have enjoyed the piano even more. At the time, piano lessons were twenty-five cents—really, twenty-five cents!

At Grandma's house, we became friends with the neighbors named the Werners. They sure could sing a yodel, but we couldn't and never did learn to do it. They and we became friends with a guitar player, so we had a great time with them. I kind of had a crush on that music man, but that is all that ever came of it. Stayed friends with the Werners and even picked potatoes with them—such many good times without drugs and/or liquor.

We had a cream separator to produce the good whole cream that everyone liked. We girls had to wash it every morning before school. Mom always took the five gallons of cream in the cream can to Backoo to sell. Wish I knew what she got for it, but she must have had some money because she would buy us one-half pint sundaes with toppings. What a treat we felt we had!

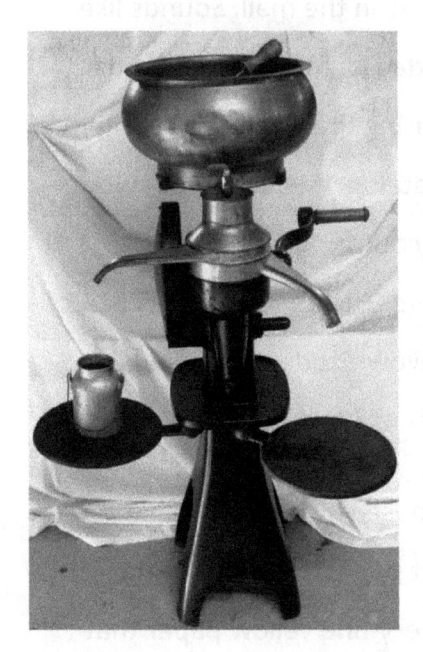

Old-fashioned cream separator. What is interesting to note is it was cranked by hand. This one has been restored, so it looks new. Fresh milk from the cow poured in the top and then crank, crank, and crank some more, and out would come cream from one spout and skim milk the other spout.

One of my chores was gathering eggs at the henhouse or watching a hen hatching little ones. Even though we had many chores around the farm, we still took time to have fun. We loved going to the Hamilton Fair each year in July. I was always lucky at bingo, so I had a few treasures from there.

A funny story here relates to the outhouse that we used as our toilet room. Every year and sometimes a few times a year, we got a huge Sears and Roebuck catalog in the mail. Sears was a major company that sold mostly items from this catalog. It was easy shopping as you filled out the order form with the item number, put it in the mail, and sooner or later your product would arrive in the mail. Sounds like the internet shopping we do today, right? This was a fine shopping experience. It is surprising the number of complete houses they sold through the catalog. If you see the two-story square house around the country, there is a good chance it was ordered from Sears. The 1940 cost was $1995 for a complete house all built. Wow—today that wouldn't buy a couch for your living room.

The catalog had another purpose you may not have guessed. It was the king of toilet paper. The back of the catalog had a section of some very fine yellow paper that was much nicer to use than the glossy paper that made up the remainder of the pages, so when the new catalog arrived, the old one was retired to the outhouse. Then here was a mad dash to get to use the yellow pages. There is a cute saying on TV now for Charmin toilet paper—"Enjoy the go"—that is what we did! It really is hard to imagine the concept of the outhouse in today's world—a small old wooden building set over top of a hole in the ground, on the inside a bench with a hole cut in it to do your duty. Cold in winter, hot in the summer!

Some pictures from the 1940 Sears and Roebuck catalog!

Our neighbors had kids younger than us. Rita and I babysat the Jensens' kids and stayed overnight. We got paid twenty-five cents each. This was a big deal for us as it was the first time we had money. One year for my birhtday, I got a pair of "saddle shoes." I thought that was a great gift. The best part was I didn't have to spend my babysitting money to buy them. You know I was known as "tight" (this was a saying in the old days meaning you were thrifty with your money and it was hard to get it from you).

I really liked school, but a bit too hard for me. I didn't pass eighth grade arithmetic state test, so I went a few months the following summer to school so I could start high school. I remember it being so hot, but I had to go. After this, I found school even harder. That same summer, I did some work for Jim Urlaub, and they would take me to the Howel barn dances. I learned to dance there. The hardest part of the job at Urlaub's was picking raspberries. I didn't mind doing the house work as they liked it to be neat, and I kept it that way. I did some sewing for the first time for myself. I made a skirt and vest and paired them with a white blouse to the barn dance. I hoped I wasn't a wallflower anymore.

I went to Cavalier for my freshman and sophmore years of high school. I hated it especially arithmetic. It was so hard for me. I will never forget bringing some homework home and asking Daddy to help me. He looked at it and said, "What the hell is that?" I understood as he never finished grade school. Also it was strange to hear him say "hell" as he never cursed.

After beginning school, I started work at a cafe in Cavalier. The wage was fifty cents an hour. I would make some good tips at twenty-five cents. It is strange to think back at how little money that is, but at the time, it was quite good. I was working with an older lady, and she wasn't very nice to me. I think it was because of my tips—but what did she expect? I walked the two miles home from work, but one night, the "taxi driver" offered to give me a ride home. All I did was pray to my guardian angel. I was so scared. Finally, after one mile, I said I would walk the last mile. I was okay, and all turned out fine.

I became friends with Grace Reopella and stayed at her house in Cavalier at times. We walked from there to high school, which was about three-quarters of a mile. It was a very cold at times. In the mornings, we made toast by holding bread over the wood fire in the stove. They had electricity in the house but, strangely, no appliances. They were very nice people, and Grace's brother liked me. Mom and Dad should have never let me date. I was just too young and trusted too much. I didn't date him very long. He wasn't handsome but was very kind.

About this time, I bought a ticket from Grandma Fritz for a chance to win a 1949 chevrolet. *The ticket cost a dollar, and I won it.* I couldn't drive it as I had no license nor money for gas or insurance. Daddy convinced me to sell it. I got $1,600 for it. As I said earlier, I was a waitress in Cavalier but now decided to quit. I had given the money to Dad, and he was my banker. I had to do a lot of explaining when I wanted some of the money. The first thing I did with the money was to buy Mom a dress. She loved it and was happy!. The rest of the money helped Mom pay for some electric things including an iron. Since there were many clothes to iron, she really loved this. The remainder of the cash was used to pay for all my school bills and had $100 left when I got married. I used that to buy a new stove.

I finished the two years of high school in Cavalier. Mom was expecting with Diane, so I did not go to school the year I would have been a junior. I stayed out to help Mom with the kids and the baby. During this summer, along with helping Mom, I also worked for Joe and Bunny Bodensteiner.

My car that cost $1.

Midge Kopf, who was a great friend, and she encouraged me to go to St. Alphonsus, my senior in 1952.

They were a great family and helped me become a better person. The following summer, I went to Grand Forks and took one and a half credits. Next, I went to St. Alphonsus in Langdon and took six and a half credits. This was perfect to graduate with the class of 1952.

I talked with Midge Kopf, who had gone to St. Alphonsus all her life, who convinced me to attend school there for my senior year. There were five of us going to school who were seniors and also Rita was attending as a freshman. Midge became one of my closest friends during this year at Saint Alphonsus.

We rented a four-room aprtment upstairs in a house in Langdon. We cooked our meals on a kerosene stove. Most meals were eaten sitting on chairs. We were quite comfortable with the kerosene stove kept us warm, but going to get fuel for the stove was a cold trip during the winter months. We went four blocks north to Sturlagsons gas stattion—no car, so everywhere we went meant walk, walk, walk. Wore pants under our skirts but took them off when we got to school, but they did keep us warm.

Things were so different then. We wore snow boots along with the long underwear and pants. They usually fit over our shoes. Always there was a real mess caused by melting snow on the linoleum as we had to keep the boots inside after we took them off. They would freeze if left outside, but if kept inside, they were warm when we needed them. The trek to school was about the same every day. I often wished I had kept the Bel Air chevy car that I had won, but once again, there was no money to operate it. Rita only attended St. Alphonsus for about six months and then decided to go home and work.

Potato truck and crew who loaded the bushel bags in the field.

Uncle Bill Fritz (one of Mom's younger brothers) raised potatoes on the farm that was owned by Grandpa and Grandma Fritz. We picked potaoes for three years for Bill.

The first year, when I was a freshman in high school, Mom, Rita, and myself picked. The next year, it was Rita and myself, and the third year, it was myself and Ronald. What we did was put twenty empty bags around our waist. Then we picked up recently dug potatoes, which were placed on the ground in the dip between rows. We picked into one-half bushel baskets. Two half bushel baskets were put into one of the bags we had around our waist. The bag was then left tied on the ground, and a truck and some other help would pick the full bags up. I picked mostly on my knees, which was easier on the back than bending over all day. It was hard work.

The only figures as to production I remember was one day Ronald and I picked a total of 410 bushels. This day they were big potatoes and a pleasure to work with. We were paid ten cents per bushel, which meant a huge sum of $41 for the day, so $20.50 each—a lot of money in those days. We also got a bonus of two cents per bushel if we stayed the season. Dad also worked loading the trucks. That was back-breaking work as you had to lift the sixty- to one-hundred-pound bags up onto the flat truck bed. We always had tomato sandwiches for lunch, and they were so good with the fresh tomatoes.

Grandma Fritz, like I mentioned earlier, was such a hard worker. She also helped pick some days. I always held such respect for her work ethic. I always hoped and prayed the wind wouldn't blow, but at times, it would, and that caused very dirty hair and skin.

Potato pickers on Uncle Bill's farm in 1946. Mom and Grandma Fritz were part of the crew. The women wore capris back then for work. A few years later, Ronald, Rita, and I worked as part of the crew.

There was always a party when potato picking was done. Like I said, it was very hard work, and the crew was glad to be done. Most of the time, it was the Stevensons and Marquart who played for us. No one danced. I loved it though. Of course, Mom wasn't there as she was home with the kids, but Rita and I really looked forward to it.

In the fall of 1950, Dad bought a farm from Romeo Metzger. The farm was located at Beaulieu, which was northeast of Olga, about four miles. According to my brother Ronald, he bought a quarter of land here, which included the entire farmstead. He paid $8,000. This seems like a small amount in today's world but was hard to justify then. The land was located almost to the bottom of a very large hill named the Beaulieu hill. The country school, located a few miles away, was also named this. I believe all the boys went to this school for a period. Ronald went to this school until he graduated eighth grade. After that, he made the decision to help Dad on the farm.

The greatest thing about the new farm was we now had electricity though still no running water and no bathroom. The outdoor potty system was still in place along with the nighttime bucket inside the hoouse. What is odd, as I said earlier, there were very few electric appliances even though there was electricity. Can you imagine that I spent my entire first eighteen years and never had running water in any of our homes. The younger crowd today will probaly find this to be unbelievable. It is true as I lived it. We just never gave it much thought as it was our life then. I have said a few times that we were happy as life was so simple back then. Even when presented with electricity, things hardly changed—unreal!

I suddenly just remembered being asked go to prom in Walhalla by Leonard Urlaub. Mom let me get a perm, but I don't remember the dress I wore. Poor Leonard and myself were completely dumb as to how the dance process worked. We didn't get dances set up before, so we sat most of the night. He was sorry, and I felt bad for him.

Back to the house, another cold house but better than the last one (Becker house). There were two rooms upstairs—one for the boys (Ronald, Melvin, Louis, and Jerry) and one for the girls (myself and Rita), one bedroom downstairs, which was Mom and Dad's, then one room for a kitchen and an attached porch where we seperated the milk and cream.

**My brother Jerry painted this picture of the house—
terribly small for Mom, Dad, and seven children!**

A couple of things that are hard to see in the picture but worth noting—left of the house is a red-colored hand pump on top of a water well. This was our only source of water, so every drop the entire family used had to be pumped by hand and hauled from here. Another item worth noting is the barrel on the left corner of the house. This caught rainwater that Mom liked to use to wash clothes. It is hard to imagine that I spent my entire life up till now without any source of running water.

It's hard to imagine today. Keep in mind here, as I talk about milk and cream, that selling the cream in town brought much-needed money for the family. The money generated usually went a long ways to paying for the grocery bill, and at times, there would be extra money to buy some treats for us, which were never enough to spoil us but enough to keep us happy. I've mentioned how different times were compared to today, but overall, life was just much simpler and enjoyable.

Larry was born Christmas Day of that year, making his birthday December 25, 1950. Like Jerry, he was born in Park River and only the second of Mom and Dad's children that were not born at home. The first crop that Dad planted on this farm was in 1951. I will always remember him talking about the soil being all gumbo. He was not very pleased with it. The definition of a gumbo soil is as follows: there is only about one hour that it is fit to farm. If it is worked too wet, it makes all lumps. If it is too dry to work, the tillage and planting cannot be done as it is as hard as a rock. Thus, there is only an hour between too wet or too dry. At least it wasn't salty like the Swanson farm. Later in life, Dad did a land trade with a neighbor and acquired better land. Thank God!

Graduated spring of 1952. Happy days!

I graduated from Saint Alphonsus High School in the spring of 1952. The Bishop Muuech presided over the ceremony as we had one of the largest graduating classes ever. Thirty three of us.(33). Wow a big class! I wish I could have gotten to know all of them earlier in time than I did. Tom Kram was one of my favorites. He never did marry. I think the nuns were also very fond of him too. Of course Mary Ann (Midge) Kopf from Leroy was my favorite girl friend.

I had no graduation party at home nor did I attend the school party at some gravel pit. Yes, I know this sounds again like a another "Walter way back story," but I wasn't into the party scene. In fact, once again, comparing then until now, many of the kids were much like myself and not so interested in the partying. I wasn't friends with the kids who were partiers. I didn't chastize the ones who did party and didn't know them very well at all.

As a high school graduation present from Mom and Daddy, I received a beautiful cedar chest shown below. I will never forget it and to this day love the smell of the cedar wood. The gift was so welcome because I had done a lot of crocheting and sewing blankets. I needed a place to keep them safe. Something simple to go along with the simplicity of life seventy-two years ago, this type of present was not uncommon as money was hard to come by. Thus, everyone got presents at graduation that were always useful but not very cool. Sorry, no new cars for our generation of kids from the farm. I suppose there were wealthy parents that gave kids cars, but I did not know of anyone. As I said a few times already, I wish it would have been possible to keep the car I won. (Now I have said it three times—LOL.)

Picture of my beautiful cedar chest.

You will see in the next part of the book how important the chest became over the years. It held so many treasures. Some years later, as I moved from large house to small house, I gave the chest away. It was a bit sad but now holds someone else's memories.

I suspected Mom and Dad didn't have enough money to send me to college. Diane was born during the summer in Park River on July 30. They were happy to have another girl after the five boys in a row. Mom and Dad now had eight children, thus adding to my thoughts of their hardship financially. I thought if I worked, then possibly I could pay for my own college. My plan started coming together in the summer of 1952. I went to work for Sid (Sylveo) and Charlotte Chaput. They lived about seven miles southwest of Langdon. They needed a girl to help on the farm and do some chores in the barn. I got up at five to help Charlotte do chores as she was expecting. She eventually lost the baby, and I was so sad.

One day, we washed clothes, and I had all the clothes I had there in the wash. I needed something to wear, so Charlotte said to wear some of her shorts. Well, I did but let me tell you they were kind of too big and not exactly cute for an eighteen-year-old girl. I'm not trying to be mean here as she was so gracious.

Now Sid and Charlotte had neighbors that lived about a quarter mile to the south. It was the Dettler family. One of the Dettlers visited Sid many mornings at milking time as they were pretty close friends. I didn't know this, but one morning after we finished milking, into the house came Sid and his friend, who just happened to be Aelred. Wow, I couldn't believe how handsome he was. At the same time, I was so embarrassed as I was wearing Charlotte's shorts. I couldn't believe the timing! Aelred came to visit every morning now at milk time. I got to know him and was smitten beyond belief. I had, at that time, a man I was calling my steady boyfriend and was engaged to be married. I had been dating him while I was going to St. Alphonsus my senior year.

Sid asked me if I thought it would be ok if they (Sid and Charlotte), Aelred and myself could go to Grafton to hear a country Western artist (Bill Anderson). Off we went, and it was like a fairy tale. Now I told myself that if I ever saw Aelred after I left my job at Chaput's, in my mind I knew I could not marry the other man.

Without phones at Chaput's or at home, I figured I would never hear from Aelred again, so I wouldn't have to worry about the decision to end my current marriage engagement. The job ended, and I returned home. I never expexted what happened next. I received a letter almost immediatley from Aelred asking me if I wanted to go to the movies in Walhalla. I said okay and couldn't get a letter mailed back to him fast enough. How God works His miracles. Now to the rest of the story.

Aelred came on Sunday night. It had rained, and our great gumbo land was living up to its reputation. Aelred got stuck with his perfectly clean car. In the process of getting out, his new black shiny shoes were full of the gumbo. I'm sure he was so embarrassed to meet Mom and Dad. My brothers all laughed like crazy at the situation.

We never made it to the movie that night, but Aelred was not to be deterred. After the fall work on the farm got done, he again asked me to the movies. The rest is history. I must say it is good that God doesn't answer all your prayers. I earlier that summer had prayed to be able to marry my steady friend before I met Aelred. Now, in this case, God answered the right one. Aelred said he and his mother were going to Boston, and he asked me if I wanted to go. I said I didn't think so. Then he said, "You could go if you changed your name to Doreen Dettler," so I did accept his proposal. He was very kind to ask my feelings about having his mother living with him. I said I was perfectly fine with that. At a later time, you will learn how important Grandma Bea was.

On the New Year's Day before our wedding, I was invited to have dinner at Aelred's house on the farm. His aunt Irene and uncle Leanard Urlaub were there too. Well, uncle put one of those fake fart things on my chair, then he dropped a spoon, and I bent over to pick it up. Then came the *pooh, pooh*—another most embarrassing moment—but everyone had a good laugh. I was learning that Aelred and his family were always pulling tricks on one another. Now I had a good feeling that the family I was marrying into were down-to-earth people.

After I had made my decision to marry Aelred, I was with Grandma Fritz sometime before the wedding. Oh boy, I got a butt chewing because I had stood up the first person I was engaed to. I pled my case, but she was still not sure of my decision. I do have to say as she got to know Aelred, she really liked him.

Spending the day at the Dettler Farm on New Years Day, 1953.

One time before the wedding, I was home on the farm. Daddy had gotten a new car. I asked him if I could borrow it to go to town. Well, he said yes. Guess what—I backed it into a tree. There was no damage, but I still had to go and tell Dad. I wasn't in too much trouble. God knows how to let us not to get too "high hatted." I have tried to be humble. Praise God!

As I end part 1 of my story, I wanted to add two more pictures. I know you've heard me say I liked school very much, but it was quite hard for me to keep my grades up. Below is my senior report card. I thought you might like to see it for a couple of reasons. One is the kinds of classes that were being taught in school then, which included things like journalism, bookkeeping, and "problems," which I guess was math. Home ec was also being taught. This class

9 Week Periods	Days Absent	Religion IV	English IV	Problems	Bookkeeping	Home Ec	Journalism	Eng. III	SCHOLARSHIP
									Excellent—A 95-100 Good —B 87-94 Average —C 80-86 Pass —D 75-79 Fail —F Below 75
1	17	B	C	B-	A-	C	B		
2	7	A	B	C	A	C	A		
Sem.			B-			B-			
3	13½	B	C	B	A	B	B	B	
4	3½	B	B-	B	B	A-	B	B	
Sem.	41	91	85	95	94	B	87	87	
			87						

PRINCIPAL

55

should have been easy as we lived and learned it at home. Second, and I'm humble here as I just wanted to show that things turned out okay in my grades. Thank you, God! I also added Aelred's graduation picture. He was only sixteen years old, and I was only six years old when it was taken! Graduated top of his class.

Part 2

1953 to 2024

Aelred and I were married on January 20, 1953. The ceremony took place at the Catholic church in Olga. It was so beautiful though small, but I was so happy and praised God!

Daddy walks with me, and we eat cake.

The wedding party for our "wee" wedding included my cousin Betty Howatt as the bridesmaid. Aelred's brother Leonard Gerald was the best man. The flower girl and ring bearer were the Plante twins—Jim and Judy. They were my Aunt Annie's children.

It was a day which is not unusual for January in northern North Dakota. A winter storm was raging. Daddy took a few things to the church, and after returning home the few miles we lived from the church, he said he did not think we would be married today. The storm eased somewhat, and Aelred was able to make it to Olga. I had picked out my wedding ring earlier when Aelred had taken me to the jewelry store in Langdon and asked me to pick one of three choices. I never asked the price but always felt that it was affordable for him—a beautiful ring! Aelred must have been extremely nervous as he forgot to bring the marriage license with him. Uncle Jerry had to brave the storm for forty-plus miles and return to the farm and then back to Olga.

Interesting to note here are the prices for my wedding gown. I paid a total of $40 for my dress, veil, and shoes then another $8 for a suit to wear on the honeymoon. Gosh, can you imagine these prices compared to today's brides? Some brides pay thousands for a dress. My son, Kevin told me of a bride spending $4,000 on a dress and did not like it. It was nonreturnable, so she had to purchase another $4,000 one. I think Daddy would have had a heart attack dealing with this scenario. I would never have dared to even return my $40 dress. My, how times have changed. I laugh as I wrote that statement as I guess the book could be called just that—*My, How Times Have Changed.*

I had stayed up the night before the wedding to take care of baby Diane so Mom could attend the wedding. She was suffering from "pleurisy," also known as some lung inflammation, and didn't feel well enough to attend. I was sad but knew Mom was praying with us on this glorious day.

God was with us that day as many people traveled quite a distance to attend, yet all were safe and warm. I was actually amazed at the turnout we had, considering the weather; but then again, we were all used to the cold snowy winters that were so common back then.

Our Lady-Sacred Heart Catholic Church, Olga, ND.

We left on our honeymoon at about 5:00 p.m. The storm had eased even further, so we started out for Dayton, Ohio. We were going to visit Aelred's sister Moira and her husband, Vince, and their family. The big cities were new to me as previously I had only been to two places. One was Winnipeg, Manitoba, Canada for our senior skip day and one time to Fargo, North Dakota. I suppose this may have been farther than Mom and Daddy had been at the time as I don't remember them going on any long trips. We were gone for about ten days on the honeymoon.

I had one bad night while we were gone. I burst out crying because I missed the little kids at home. I was glad when Aelred told me he understood. I felt so bad and hoped he wasn't wondering if he had married a "preteen." It was one of the few times I cried. I had also wished while on the trip that a telephone call would have been available to contact Mom to see how she was doing, but since there was no telephone at Daddy and Mom's house, we had no idea how it was going.

We didn't cover many miles each day. I guess I blame it on "love." I remember going through Indianapolis. The streetlights continued for miles, and it seemed like there was no end to them. I was impressed as back home we had zero lights. In fact, we were lucky to have cars on the street most of the time. Vince and Moira were glad to see us. Next, we visited my uncle Ernest and aunt Malvina Lepire in Michigan. She gave us a "basket-pattern quilt" that was a very nice wedding gift. On a side note, in those days, there was no such thing as being "registered" for wedding presents. People generally gave handmade presents that proved to be very functional and truly needed.

Then we went back to Indiana to visit Aelred's cousins, the Deiners. They were very gracious to us. Many milk cows kept them very busy along with a very large grain business where they sold seed and other things. Then it was back home to the farm in Perry township, south of Langdon, North Dakota—a big adventure for a young gal from Olga.

On day number three, Aelred asked why I was only eating toast for breakfast. I explained that I had no idea of knowing if we had any more money than that to pay for food. He laughed and assured me the answer was yes.

We had money for food! The next page gives some good figures as to the cost of things when we got married. Thank God they were cheaper than today. Looking at the below chart, it's interesting to note that the average income people earned for just a little over two years would buy a new

1953 Cost of Living

LIVING

New House	$9,525.00
Average Income	$4,011.00 per year
New Car	$1,651.00
Average Rent	$83.00 per month
Tuition to Harvard University	$600.00 per year
Movie Ticket	70¢ each
Gasoline	20¢ per gallon
First-Class Postage Stamp	3¢ each

FOOD

Granulated Sugar	85¢ for 10 pounds
Vitamin D Milk	94¢ per gallon
Ground Coffee	76¢ per pound
Bacon	55¢ per pound
Eggs	24¢ per dozen
Fresh Ground Hamburger	54¢ per pound
Fresh Baked Bread	16¢ per loaf

house—little chance of that working today. A loaf of bread for sixteen cents—wow!

It seems during this period, people had enough money to travel again compared to the years after World War II and the Great Depression. I was really worried about finances back then as I wasn't used to spending any money of consequence. Aelred proved to be very aligned with my conservative ways. I was glad of this fact as I was used to Mom and Daddy's relationship being one of mutual conservative ways. I really had no one else to compare with, so I guess I was seeing what I expected.

The following picture is the farm as it looked back around 1915. It was a welcome sight after returning home from the honeymoon. In the next few weeks, I was able to grasp what my jobs would be around the farm. I was used to hard work and long hours, so I wasn't scared to tackle anything. I only knew I wanted to work next to Aelred and do all I was asked.

Dettler Farmstead built in the early 1900s.

Aelred was always very kind and never pressured me to help. The house was huge and had both running water and electricity. Wow, I thought I had hit the big time.

Aelred's father, Leonard, had passed away when he was only fifty-two. I never had a chance to meet him. He was a smoker, quite overweight, but loved life. He was constantly playing tricks on everyone, especially his relatives.

Aelred's parents: Leonard Dettler and Bea Fitz Gerald.

Aelred's mother, Beatrice or Bea, as everyone called her, lived at the house also. Before we were married, Aelred had been nice to ask me if it was okay for his mother to be living at the house after we were married. I had agreed to it, and it was the right decision. She must have loved us so much. The reason I say that is because living with us must have been hard. She continued to live with us even as her husband was gone and she didn't want to live alone. Sometimes she would go away for the winter and stay with one of her other four children or go to Boston or Prince Edward Island, Canada, where she had brothers and sisters.

Grandma Bea's home on Prince Edward Island, Canada. She came from a large family.

    She was a huge help with the children. She taught them so much. I was so busy with all the work of the little kids, gardening, milking cows, farming, or baking. Grandma Bea took on some of the responsibility of teaching. When she first came to the United States, she was a teacher by trade and had been in Saskatchewan teaching, so it was natural for her, and I was so glad. She was an angel at night, a poor sleeper, so she always knew when the children came home. Of course, she would report that to me as I wouldn't know as I was a sound sleeper, but I was so thankful for the extra sleep!

Grandma Bea was so good at fixing leftovers the best and used them all. Her biscuits were also the best as she made them with cream. I always remember what she served when Aelred brought me to meet her before we were married. It was ham and scalloped potatoes, California salad—which I loved then and still do—pickles, and for dessert, she had made apple pie with a slice of cheese on it. Wonderful!

When we got back from the honeymoon, Grandma Bea was getting ready to go to her daughter Moria's home in Dayton, Ohio. She said to me, "Doreen, I give you everything here in this home—it's all yours." How in the world could I refuse this—a beautiful home with all I would ever want, especially the electric stove and an actual bathroom.

The marriage and the honeymoon were so wonderful. As the farming season started, I worked keeping track of income and expenses for the farm in our record book. Aelred said this was a great help. Some folks from Olga surprised us one night. It was a nice party with lunch, and they were all great people.

It wasn't long after this that I went to the doctor. I came home and told Aelred we were expecting. It brought such joy on December 28th when Kevin was born. Everything was perfect.

I made a big change for this year as I started going to St. Alphonsus Church in Langdon with Aelred. He and his family had been going there since it was built. They were long-standing Catholics in the community.

St. Alphonsus Church in Langdon, North Dakota.

1954

As Aelred and I started our second year of marriage, I couldn't be any happier. Baby Kevin seemed to be very good. We did not have any fights over money or spending. There was enough to cover the farm expenses and the living costs for the following people: Aelred's grandparents Otto and Nell (they lived in Langdon), Grandma Bea, Aelred, and me. We all wrote checks from the same bank account. It all worked out to be okay. The bank was also easy to work with.

I am going to provide some very interesting information on the following pages. This information is somewhat boring, but it fits with my theme of providing the reader with facts from the "Walter way back years." As I said earlier, one of my new jobs around the farm was to keep track of income and expenses for the farm. The first picture is of the record book that many local farms used to track business money. The book was provided free from Chuck Skabo, who owned the Coast-to-Coast store in Langdon. This store was very similar to today's True Value stores. They were great for bolts, supplies, and small hardware parts. I have added many pictures taken from this record book. My goal here is to provide not only numbers that will seem almost so low as to be unbelievable but also give you a sense of how little income was produced on the farm per year. The two sources of income were crop sales and the cream and egg money.

The record book we used. They were available every year. This record keeping was all new to me as I was never involved with Mom and Dad's farm numbers.

GRAIN AND SEEDS SOLD
During This Year

Month	Date	Kind	Quan.	Sold to	Amount		Month	Date	Kind	Quan.	Sold to
Mar	9	Ob	200	F&G&M	122	36					
Jul	5	Bar	386	"	345	00					
Aug	6	Bar	149	"	118	65					
Aug	9	CC		C.C.C.	202	94					
"	28	"		"	506	57					
Nov	15	Flax	957	Farmers Co-op Elevator	2485						
Sept	29	Wht	34	F&G&M	28	00					
"	25	Bly	1456	F U G M	1679	25					
Oct	15	Flax	343	"	1029	00					
Nov	18	Bly	871		1001	00					

**The grain income for the entire 1954 year.
The total is $7,053.26.**

Here we see we raised oats, barley, flax, and spring wheat. Look at the prices per bushel. Oats were $.60 per bushel. Barley was around $1 per bushel. Wheat was $2 per bushel. Lastly, flax was the big cash crop at $3 per bushel. With these kind of low prices, the farm needed to produce large quantities of these crops, but yields were very low on farms. Commercial fertilizers were used sparingly.

Here we have an additional $506.69 (about $10/week) from cream and egg sales, bringing the total farm income for the year to $7,559.89.

Now keep in mind this $7,599.89 kept Aelred, me, and the baby operating and living for the entire year along with Grandpa Otto and his wife, Nell, and Grandma Bea. It almost seems impossible. This was and still is a real eye-opener for me.

These are the expenses to fix the farm equipment for the year. The total of $239 defies belief. In 2023, it's impossible to buy a five-gallon pail of motor oil for that. We never owned a welder on the farm, so some of this expense included hiring someone to weld, Julius Thon in Langdon. It looks like the John Deere dealer in Langdon called Hughes and Work got used for new parts, along with Liebler Implement.

This page shows money spent on supplies. This category usually contained smaller less-expensive parts like bolts, belts, or lumber. Some of this category could contain large new items bought like a new freezer at $130 or a hydraulic hoist for the truck box at $440. This is another amazing total here of $783.

I wanted to show a page of the household expenses. This section shows $514. The amounts spent on each visit to the stores are so small. There is an entry for $.10 cents. Wow!

I showed most of the important categories of expenses from the book. I'm sorry if I bored you with these pages of numbers. It was just so important to me to know the details of how much we made and how much we spent. It's funny that as the years went by, I gradually stopped paying attention so much to the details, but I knew in my heart when things were out of line. I still continued to be very conservative even as farm profits increased somewhat. The category above shows *$514* for the entire period, including mostly amounts spent on groceries and all supplies related to the household. I don't have to tell you that today, that $514 would buy hardly a couple of grocery bags of groceries. At that time, I felt I was spending too much. I will bet young couples starting out today are thinking the very same—too much money for groceries and household expenses.

Lastly, I wanted to show the page for hired labor. This page was not in as good a shape as the others so is harder to read. We usually hired one of my brothers to do field work. I remember Melvin working for sure. We would also hire at different times one of the Hansel boys. Dennis and Jimmy worked for sure at times. The Hansels were always such good friends and so kind. They made life easier and more fun. They lived just a half mile away, so we spent much time there.

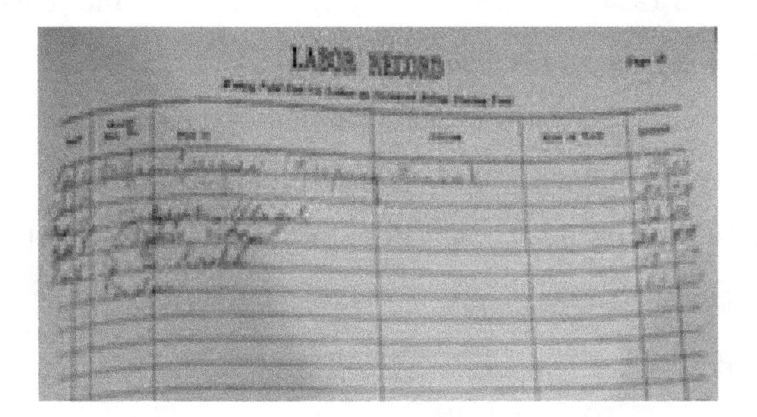

The total labor for the year was $194.

Who could you possible hire for that amount? Granted, we didn't need a full time man so this was just some part-time labor. The farm consisted of about six hundred acres then with maybe half planted to crops. The rest consisted of pastures and slough areas that weren't drained. This was a bit larger than some locally, but still we were able to do most of it ourselves.

One of my classes in high school was bookkeeping. I was glad to have taken the class but at times wished my memory of what I was taught would have stayed longer. The record book was well organized and helped me tremendously.

So this ends my 1954 bookkeeping. I am so glad Aelred had faith in me to keep track of all of this. People that lived through 1954 understand perfectly, and many of the years following that farms did not produce huge amounts of income. We had very little excess money; thus, as stated earlier, we didn't go many places. Visiting relatives was by far the most common activity because it was relatively inexpensive to do. Played cards and horse shoes—the simple life.

I was finding the neighbors to all be great. Like I said earlier was the Hansels. There was also Sid and Charlotte Chaput and their kids whom you heard of before. In just a few square miles around the farm, we also had the Borhos, Delvos, Gellners, more Chaputs, and Waltzes. We all helped one another where needed, and they were always eager to help. This fact was so welcome. You never know what kind of impression you make with people when you are new in any group, but it seemed I fit in!

The following happened to make me feel good. We mowed the grass up next to the house with a push mower that had a drum of sharp knives that was turned by pushing the mower. It was hard when the grass would get too tall, so Charlotte said we should pool our cream checks together and buy an actual push mower that was gas driven. We did buy one and took turns using it. We eventually bought our own. I was happy that she thought enough of me to be a partner. There were many other instances when Aelred would work together with Sid and/or Joe at harvest time. No one did any keeping track of hours or acres, which kept it so friendly.

Aelred's grandma Nell passed away at the end of the year. Grandpa Otto remained in Langdon. He eventually couldn't take care of himself and moved out to the farm with Aelred and me. He had terrible headaches caused by high blood pressure. He had a mild stroke and couldn't take his medications properly.

He hated the idea of his grandson Aelred going to Mass in the Catholic Church. One time he threw the crucifix across the bedroom because he was upset. At one time, he had been a Mason, and he was definitely an atheist. This made it so hard for us to take care of him as everyone around him was a devout Catholic. He also would pee in the wash sink but not the sink for dishes. He was a very round man and eventually was hospitalized before death as home care was not possible anymore.

Just a note here—I spent most of my married life with some family member or members living with us at the house: Otto for a number of years, Grandma Bea for almost twenty years, Aelred's brother Gerald for a number of years after Grandma Bea passed away. It wasn't until we moved into Langdon that we were alone in the house—a very welcome relief. Of course, there were times of loneliness after all the years of house guests, but it still was nice for Aelred and I to be alone.

Aelred's Grandpa Otto Dettler and Grandma Nellie.

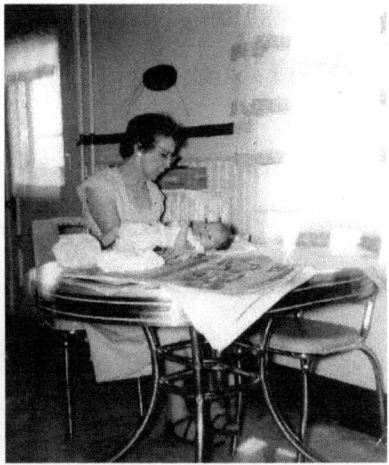

Grandma Bea before marriage and also taking care of baby Kevin.

1955

Mary Beth joined us on January 6th. I was so happy to have a daughter. All was perfect! As she grew up, she was a mini-me. She was never afraid to work, and her devotion to the Lord was a lifetime commitment for her. She was probably the one child who commanded the respect of the others. She was never in any trouble and was always obedient. If she was to be home at 10:00 pm, she would be early, never late for anything all through her life. She liked to tease a little using her dry humor but was always kind. The worst thing that happened to her when young was when

Kevin was riding a snowmobile rather foolishly and ran into her and broke her leg.

She was a very good student also. She loved to watch NFL football and could converse with the boys about players and game strategy.

1956

Steven was born June 25th. Mom also had twin girls Corriene and Connie this year. This now made a total of ten children for Mom and Daddy. It was nice that the twins were the age of our children as they loved to play together. They were together often as we either went to Mom and Daddy's or they were at the farm with us.

The interesting part of their birth is it is now twenty-two years after I was born. I'm hoping my writing here will compare how things are so much different for them versus my youth.

I always thought the boys, including Steven, were more like me. The girls seem more like Aelred with their joke-telling ability. Steven, before he learned to walk, used to scoot around on the floor on his butt. He would use his legs to pull himself forward, and he was so fast.

1957

Another baby boy, Chalmer, was born on August 30th. He was the heaviest of the four children born so far—another good baby—and everything was perfect.

1958

David was born August 29. Everything was perfect again. A funny story happened the day after he was born. It was harvesting time, and Aelred and Joe Hansel were combining in the same field. I had to take lunch to the field for everyone. Grandma Bea usually came along to help distribute lunch, and we would also have lunch in the field. Thus, the kids came with us in the car. We loaded the car and headed down the road and realized we had forgotten to bring the baby. They were all so little, so we thought we had all five of them. I prayed I would never do that again.

In July of this year, we had an opportunity to buy some land. It was three quarters, or 480 acres. It was located south and west of the farm, about six miles in north Loma

Township. The Kapreva family owned it and offered to sell it to us for a little over $50 per acre. This amounted to $24,160 total. This was a huge amount of money in 1958. I had a really hard time grasping just how much money this really was. Aelred and I prayed and asked for some scenario that would allow us to buy the land. We were currently keeping up with the expenses on the farm but had very little excess spending money. Now with five children, our thoughts overall were to pass on the opportunity.

The Kapreva family seemed to take a liking to our family. There were six of them in total that were the owners of the land. It appeared that Clarence was the major decision-maker. He came to us with a proposal. He expressed that he had talked with the rest of his family, and they had decided to offer a contract for deed (CFD). He said all we needed was to put $5,000 down for the down payment, and they would finance the remaining $19,160. Wow, okay, that was some wonderful news. The payment was to be $2,000 for ten years starting in the fall of 1958 after the crop was harvested then another nine payments for the years 1958 through 1967 then a final payment of $1,1160.34 in 1968. That was it—simple, right?

The terms the Kaprevas were offering could possibly work except for one huge problem. Where do we get the $5,000 for the down payment? A few days later, we were visiting Mom and Daddy, and the subject of the land came up. I'm not sure exactly how it came about—whether we asked or Daddy offered to loan us the money—but we did get a loan from him for the $5,000. We were so thankful and pledged to pay him back. We praised God for his assistance, and we made the decision to purchase the land. I will tell you it was a great decision, but you have no idea how hard it was to make the payment every year to both parties, but we did. I know today that most people would enjoy owning 480 acres for a paltry sum of $2,500 per year, but that is how things have changed.

Aelred began work on the Loma farm, as we called it, after the crop was harvested at home. He thought he counted over forty potholes or sloughs on the three quarters. He bought a new two-and-a-half-yard dirt scraper to dig some drainage ditches to drain some of the potholes. Thus began thirty very long days for him as he worked until the ground froze up cutting ditches. It seemed endless so here hired the Mickelson brothers from Langdon to come with some of their huge equipment to cut some of the really big ditches. He then would provide the smaller ones. This turned out to be a yearly project and was well worth all the effort.

The land at home was rocky, but it was nothing compared to the Loma farm. It seemed every time a chisel plow or cultivator ran through it, more and more rocks were appearing. This eventually got better after about ten years but not perfect. The children and I spent many hours over the years picking rocks.

Ronald and Rosanna got married on November 8 this year. I was a bridesmaid. Aelred took pictures with a movie camera to produce the memory on film. As we knew we would be busy, I asked my brother Jerry to watch Kevin, Mary Beth, and Steven. During the Mass, Steven had to go to the bathroom. Jerry kept putting him off, hoping to get to the end of the ceremony. First thing, I'm at the front of the church at the altar, and I see pee running down from the pew where the kids are sitting. I didn't get much out of the Mass as I was so embarrassed. Jerry felt so bad. After Mass, we got Steven dressed in some of Artie Brusseau's clothes. He wore them the rest of the day and evening. Thank God, the

Brusseaus lived in Olga where the wedding was. Had a great time and danced all night!

1959

Kevin started school this year. He didn't like it and used to cry every morning before he left the farm. He was so used to going to the field with Aelred. I was surprised he missed that even though he would sit on the tractor, combine or swather out in the open for days that were at least ten hours. Oh, the bugs, dirt, and hot temperatures. I guess he was a farmer early in life. There were no school buses when he was in first grade, so Sid's older daughter and her boyfriend would load Kevin in the back seat and drive to school in Langdon. I learned some years later how much he hated that also.

1960

We were blessed again this year with the birth of Joni. Her birthday was February 25. We were so happy to have another daughter. Love had been constant in our marriage as a little one had joined us almost every year. Love continued, but God made the decision to let us stay at six children. I will tell of Aelred's sister Joan and her husband as they went on to have thirteen—eleven births, one miscarriage, and one stillbirth. God has a reason, and someday we will know why! We also bought a new car this year. It was huge but needed to hold all six children.

1960 Chevrolet four-door Impala.

I'm not sure if this is the exact car, but it was a big four-door. Even though it's big, if we had today's rules about seat belts and car seats back then, we still couldn't have taken all eight of us together. It's no wonder in the later years, when Chevrolet introduced their even bigger vehicles like the Suburban, that they were so popular. We were blessed to have never had even one car accident when the seat belts and car seats weren't needed that time. We were lucky.

You just can't imagine the fights and quarrels that can happen with six kids in the back seat, or at least when they were going between the back and front seats. There was no such thing as buckling in back then, so the harder we tried to keep them quiet, the more boisterous they would become. Many Sundays we went to visit my parents. This was about forty-five minutes to an hour one way. We weren't five miles down the road when we heard the following statements: "Mom, he or she is touching me" or "Mom, he or she is looking at me" or "I'm hungry." We usually would give in and give them some candy or something to occupy them for a moment, but soon it was back to the squabbling.

1961

I found a time when I could get all six children stopped long enough to get a picture! As you can imagine, this was no easy task. Without some help from Grandma Bea, this picture would not have happened. The kids were always full of energy.

From the left: David, Mary Beth, Steven, Kevin holding Joni, Chalmer.

Looking back, I remember they were all early risers in the morning. Many times, they would all be up and playing around 5:30. I usually put them to bed even as early as 8:30 as this would give me some time to myself to accomplish some daily chores such as picking and canning veggies or making jams. No wonder they were up so early, right? I did manage to get them together for another picture. It was bath time, and I lucked out again.

Joni up front. From left to right: David, Mary Beth, Chalmer, Kevin, Steven. Our version of an outdoor swimming pool on the farm!

I suppose in today's world, this picture would be chastised by certain people; but back then, this was perfectly acceptable. I would imagine there were very few times in life that I was politically correct. It seemed in our early days, people could "take a joke," as we called it. What a wonderful world it was then.

We didn't go out much when the children were little, but we did go to Fred and Chelta's Wagon Wheel café in

Langdon. The children loved it and always had hamburgers and french fries, which were just coming into menu items then. We were always on pins and needles as to how the kids would behave, but Fred and Chelta praised us for the good children. We were so proud of them!

I don't want to sound mean here, but one thing I always said was, "After the last one goes to school, I am sleeping late in the mornings." Ha, that never happens with a farm life; but with the school buses that started taking kids to school sometime in these years, we didn't have to drive to school twice a day, which allowed for a little rest during the day.

From this point on in my story, I won't be relying on any certain date in time although there will be some dates that will be listed. One story I would like to share here happened in 1982.

Mary Beth had his first child as Melissa was born that year. With her birth, we now had five generations of women. It made news in the Langdon newspaper called the *Cavalier County Republican*. From there, it was picked up by someone in the political world finally reaching the desk of our then

United States Senator Quentin Burdick. The following is a copy of a letter we received from his office—quite nice of him to take the time to respond to us especially without having to ask!

> QUENTIN N. BURDICK
> NORTH DAKOTA
>
> United States Senate
> WASHINGTON, D.C. 20510
>
> *Congratulations on a fine family!*
>
> *Quentin Burdick, U.S.S.*

This is a nice place to talk a little about politics. Aelred and I were both conservatives and voted as Republicans. As I mentioned earlier, I was glad for this. In the day there were many farmers that were Democrat only because they believed that when the Democrats were in charge in Washington DC, they received better treatment. In my heart, I didn't believe that then; and for sure in today's world, it is not true. It is very seldom that Democrats today even mention farmers!

CECILIA DOREEN DETTLER

The five generations pictured here are Grandma Fritz, seated, holding Melissa (Mary Beth's daughter); Mary Beth in the middle; myself on the left; and Mom on the right.

Thank you, Senator Burdick, for your letter.

My children are so important to me, and I love them all dearly, but I am going to talk about them a little less here in this forum than maybe some people would expect. They have wonderful lives, and I guess I will leave them to tell their own stories.

In 1963 we started a remodel of the farmhouse. As I wasn't familiar with things done previously to the house, I couldn't really appreciate all we were doing. It turned out so beautiful. Some things that were, let's say, "not so great" were fixed with the remodel.

The project included removing the third floor, which was an attic, and replacing the roof with a modern low pitch. I will never forget Aelred and Joe Hansel high in the air cutting the four sides apart and pulling them down from the top with a chain and tractor. Now we have a more functional third floor, and it is easier to heat as new insulation was added.

The house was originally built with all four bedrooms on the second level. The only bathroom was also on that level, so the new plan was to add a second bathroom and bedroom on the main level plus a one-stall garage. Previously there was no garage, so adding one stall was quite an addition. The project went well and was so welcome. Aelred and I took the first-floor bedroom. Grandma Bea had her own room upstairs, Kevin and Steven shared a bedroom, Mary Beth and Joni shared the middle room, and Chalmer and David had the remaining bedroom. One day, thoughts went back to the days of living in all those small houses before I was married. As you've learned sometimes, we had six to eight children sharing a couple of rooms. I felt so blessed!

We also expanded the leaving room by taking out some of the sliding doors that divided the big living room into smaller rooms. This made such a huge difference. It was hard to remove the doors as they were such beautiful wood and were designed as pocket doors. I spent many hours with a spatula smoothing out the plaster on the ceiling. I was actually pretty good at this.

Lastly, with this remodel, we added a room at the entrance of the house. We used this as what today they call a mud room. It was part of the garage and was accessed by a door from the garage. We also put plumbing in to allow for the washer and dryer to occupy the room. Now we had it all.

Grandma Bea was giving a tour to friends when the house was almost finished.

The ladder on the side of the house brings up a great memory. This story came out a few years after the picture was taken. It seemed the kids would climb out form the window on the second floor located on the southeast side of the house, next scoot down the roof of the garage then down the ladder. Then it was into one of their cars, which they would push down the road, then start after beyond hearing range and then go to town.

In 1968, kids were getting close to using the "ladder."

I also wanted to mention here that 1963 is the year we lost President Kennedy—of course, a shock to the world. He was actually a relative of Aelred's. Grandma Bea's family were the Fitz Gerald's as was President Kennedy's mother's family. Rose Kennedy was a Fitz Gerald before marrying Joe Kennedy, thus making Aelred a pretty close cousin. Didn't know them at all, but the connection was there. Always wished they might send a little *ca-ching* our way. LOL.

This is a good time to tell you about our summertime visitors. Aelred had three sisters: Moria, Joan, and Ellen. They and their husbands, Vince, Kermit, and Ed, would arrange to take all their vacations at the same time during the summer. They all would save their vacation time to return to the farm. The sisters had all grown up here so loved to return. This was all lovely in thought but not so in reality. Our family was a total of nine people (Aelred, me, the six kids, and Grandma Bea). Then came Moria with seven, Joan with at least twelve, and Ellen with seven—thus, the total of thirty-five lovely souls. Ed and Ellen didn't make it every year, but the rest did, so there were twenty-eight total most years.

I'm sure you can only imagine all the goings on with that many people at the house for two weeks. The amount of food consumed by all the children was crazy. It seemed we baked bread every day. Meals were made in five-gallon roasting pans. Hot dishes, pork and beans, and hot dogs were some of their favorites, sometimes even more bread as we made cinnamon rolls. There were pancake days, which required almost fifty pancakes just for the kids. The washing machine seemed like it ran day and night. The toilets were in constant use even though the outside outhouse took up some of the slack. (Yes, the Sears catalog was still available for wiping!)

The sleeping arrangement was for all (twenty-six) or (twenty-one) kids to sleep on the living room floor. Surprisingly, this went maybe better than expected as they were outside playing ball or other things all day, thus tired at night. A few were instigators of mischief but not bad. There were literally enough kids to have some really good baseball teams and games. Moria's kids, which came from Dayton, Ohio, were probably the most sports oriented of the bunch, but the rest learned from them. Our kids probably had the least experience with sports but sure knew a lot about farming though!

I am thinking of a few stories on the farm that fit here. One day it was lunch time, and Aelred was in the field running the field cultivator. I thought I would be nice and offered to run the tractor while he ate lunch. I worked for close to an hour, but I forgot to put the cultivator in the ground. I was so embarrassed. I thought I was better off at home cooking. Aelred didn't say a word, but I don't think I offered to run it again.

Aelred and I had very few misunderstandings. The most notable one was over chickens. Grandma Bea and I decided we would sell the extra chickens we had, but Aelred felt we sold them too cheap. I couldn't believe our first argument was over a few chickens!

One day I offered to pick stones at the Loma farm with the rock picker. The kids were with me, and all was going well as they were working and not arguing. One time I started the tractor moving forward and David was sitting on the front of the picker. His leg got caught, and he got run over. Steven ran to get the car at the end of the field, and off to the hospital we went. He would pass out once in a while, and I thought he was dying. Dear God, how I prayed. In the end, he had a broken shoulder. We were lucky as the ground was soft and he was simply pushed into the soft soil. The bucket was empty, also making the load lighter. This was the last of my stone-picking days.

One time I was hauling grain from the combine to the yard. I was wearing a pair of culottes, and they got caught in the elevator belt. They were ripped off, and I got a big gash in my leg. I went to the hospital, but it turned out to be less than a disaster. I questioned why I would wear such an outfit to unload grain—not very smart. Speaking of grain hauling, I was continually saved by Anna Mae Hansel. She was a tough woman, which was required to start the motor on the grain auger. I could hardly reach the belt to pull and get the motor started. Most times I would wait with my load in the yard until she showed up and got it started for me so I could unload. What a lifesaver. The combiners had to wait a little while for me, but what do you expect for free help, right?

I made lunches for Aelred and the boys when they were in the field. In those days, there were no water jugs. What I did was fill clean Hilex jugs (the name for chlorine products bought in the store) half full of water and then freeze them, in the morning fill with water, and this would last all day without thawing. Some days the water would all be gone, but there was still ice.

Earlier I said when all the children were in school, I would be able to take a little time for myself. Well, that plan didn't work so well. A little later, I decided on a new plan. After they were all done with school and moved out of the house, I would get my relaxation time. Well, guess what—that plan also sizzled. It seemed when they actually were all gone, I was sad. I started to take on projects that took my mind off my loneliness. Over the years that followed, I tried many things. Aelred helped with some of the undertakings. I had partners for some ventures, and some I did as an individual.

I'm not sure about the details that happened to cause me to start this first business. Evidently someone thought I would make a great "Avon Lady." Quite honestly, I was shocked as I just never considered myself pretty enough to sell beauty products, but I did, and it was quite fun. The timing of this business was right. The town of Langdon quadrupled in size almost overnight. The US government had decided they would build two antiballistic missile defense systems in the area. One was located at Nekoma, North Dakota, and the other at Concrete, North Dakota. The plan was to spend over one billion dollars on these two projects. That is a huge boost to our economy. The population of Langdon exploded from two thousand residents to almost eight thousand.

I don't want to say the new people in town were more uppity up than our permanent residents, but the wages they were earning seemed incredible for the time. This gave them lots of money for new cars, great clothes, and certainly beauty products to help keep up their image.

I started slowly by having sales meetings with the neighbors as I was comfortable around them. They were conservative, thus making them a pretty hard sell for my products. As I met more of the new people that had moved to town, I expanded to include them. Most of them were very cordial and bought more freely. I liked that. They would order, and the next week I would deliver their orders to them. One summer, I was sick and had to have surgery at the Mayo clinic in Rochester, Minnesota. Steven helped to deliver orders for me while I was gone. Thank you! I'm not sure he enjoyed it, but he was kind to do it. A thought comes to mind about Steven. In our day, a belt or wooden spoon was used for discipline. I never did punish the kids much but do remember using the spoon on him when he didn't want to help do dishes. That was the worst punishment I ever gave the children. I felt so bad as it still stayed in my memory. I am so sorry, Steven.

I had quite a few clients who resided in the Nekoma area and worked at the missile site. One day, I was in Nekoma delivering products to a client. I went to the door, and when my client opened it, her dog bolted out the door. Well, I've seen some mad people, but she was yelling at me, yelling at the dog, and just plain yelling. I was on the point of tears. I held onto the order I was about to deliver and left. I didn't even have a chance to tell her that I was at the wrong house. As it turns out, she was married to the general in charge of the entire project there at Nekoma. I would have thought she might be a little more cordial given their prominence, but I was wrong. I made it a point to never go back to their house.

I think I stayed with the Avon sales for about two and a half years. I made so much money I had to quit—only kidding! There may have been a few people that thought this was true. Kevin had started farming with us in 1975. Steven joined about 1977. Steven and Barb were married the next year. We decided to allow them the house on the farm, and we moved.

The farm in 1978.

No, the Avon sales didn't pay for it! The moving and building involved most of our time, so I stopped the Avon sales then. I really enjoyed it, and I think people also were glad to have had access to the products. So in 1978, our great friend and neighbor Joe Hansel started again building for us—this time a new house. It was located a mile east of the farm and west side of North Dakota Highway 1. That put us six miles south of Langdon. Aelred helped Joe every day. The children who were able to take some time also helped. Joe was so talented, and he did it all. He even built some things inside. We had a full basement, and he also did the work there too. During the entire process, I was amazed that with proper planning and hard-working people, the house was completed in record time.

The new house on a beautiful winter day.

There were setbacks—one, I remember, was a basement wall collapsing for some reason. Luckily, no one was badly hurt. We had a few parties in the new basement. Playing card games was always the guests' favorite. We had whist tournaments but very few pinochle players. The consumption of alcohol was very low compared to modern-day parties—more coffee than anything else.

About this time, I learned that my brother Melvin was sick and fighting cancer. I was so sad and prayed for his victory to win the battle. Here is an updated picture of the family.

Front row: Diane, Corriene, Connie. Rita and I are in the middle. The boys, left to right: Ronald, Louis, Jerry, Melvin, Larry.

Before I leave the story of the new house, I would like to relate a bittersweet event from September 1978. We pushed hard to be able to finish the house before winter. We were so happy with our progress, but Mother Nature dealt a terrible blow. The wheat crops that year were some of the best we had raised in the last five years. We had swathed three hundred acres, and it was lying on the ground, waiting to be harvested as we worked on the house. A storm came along with a huge amount of hail and wiped out the entire acreage. We were devastated. This was truly a mind-numbing disaster. The boys were so disappointed as they felt they should have been combining instead of working on the house. As we prayed, we realized that God's plan for dealing this blow was not to be understood now.

In these situations, it's easy to lose faith, but we didn't, and God continued to help in other ways!

Maybe this crop loss was an inspiration for me to try the many businesses that I undertook over the next forty-plus years. As I look back from now, I'm not sure how they all started. It wasn't like I sat down and did business plans and profit and loss projections like what happens today. I just would plunge in. So off I went.

I enjoyed the Avon business. Sally Stremick, who was the local Mary Kay products dealer, asked me to try selling Mary Kay under her. You know it was pretty good, and I actually enjoyed selling it again. Sally was very respected, thus making it easy to follow in her steps. There was still a scattering of the people still working on the missile defense program, so I still had that edge. I worked on this for some years and then moved on to other ideas. I'm not writing all these stories to bring praise to myself but to show I like to be busy. Aelred was fifty-two years old when he started to retire from farming, and I was forty-two years old. Now after the house was built, he was pretty much out of the farming, so I was too young to sit around and do nothing.

One of the fun things we did in 1971 before Aelred's complete retirement from farming was to take a trip to Hawaii. Aelred and I were going along with Mom and Daddy. My brother Jerry was stationed in Honolulu as he served in the Air Force. We thought it would be a great trip to visit him. It was exciting to do the planning. Our dilemma proved to be the fact that none of us had flown on an airplane previously. The apprehension built as the date of departure approached. I don't know who was more afraid, Daddy or Aelred. In the end, we drove to Los Angeles and flew from there to Honolulu.

Hawaii beach, 1971, but staying away from water.

Mom and Daddy with matching Hawaiian garb.

Of all the stories I remember was Daddy looking out the window and seeing the airplane wings going up and down as we were experiencing some turbulence. He thought they were moving twenty feet. I think they move some, but not that much. He thought he would never get home. It was a good trip, and we were true tourists and spent time at sites like Pearl Harbor. Time was also spent on the beach but not in the water as most of us were also afraid of the water. We didn't take any boat rides either. I'm sure all these fears were generated by our upbringing on the farms. The above pictures were taken there. The trip home after returning to Los Angeles included visiting some of Daddy's and Mom's relatives who lived in California. Lots of fun. We did make a quick trip through Las Vegas, but as I remember, none of us was too impressed with the town. We couldn't figure out what all the hype was about. It would be some forty-eight years before I saw it again.

My next idea to stay busy was to sell some jewelry. For this business, I worked with a partner in Carol. She was Steven's wife, Barb's mother. We sold some pretty nice things for the time period. We got along great as her kids were also gone from home. This allowed us both the time needed to have the meetings or parties, as we called them, and fill and deliver orders. It really worked well as when we had parties, I could double up and sell some beauty products and jewelry at the same time. I want to say the company was Sarah Coventry Jewelry.

A piece of jewelry we sold—nice cross with a heavy chain.

    I'm not sure of all the dates for beginning and ending these previous ventures nor the next one. I do know that some of these were going on at the same time. The next business I did with my good friend Donna Waltz. I have no idea where the idea came from, but we started making doll clothing. This is going to seem crazy, but we were making this clothing to put over the top of Air Wick air fresheners. Our feeling was that it would cover those fresh air products as they sat in people's houses, the Air Wicks were then invisible. Below are some pictures of our dolls.

Pictures of dolls used over Air Wicks.

We sold these at craft fairs in Cando, Walhalla, Munich, and Cavalier. Donna had a store on the main street of Langdon, so we sold them there also. The cost was $1 to make, and we sold them for $7. Usually I sewed the clothes and Donna would build the heads. We had different talents—a pretty unique idea for sure. I will bet there are still some of these hiding in some of our customers' closets. They could still be used as the air fresheners are still available at stores.

I was busy. Not only was I doing all this selling, but I also was busy making quilts and afghan blankets. I made hundreds of these. First, I made some for our kids. Then I made some for all the grandkids, then the great grandkids, then my brothers and sisters, then it was their kids and family, then it was the ones for raffle tickets at different charities. Like I say, it was in the hundreds when I was all done. Oh, did I mention I was also crocheting doilies. Then there were the baby blankets and burp cloths that numbered in the hundreds. It seemed for about the last thirty years, my fingers and my sewing machine have never stopped. Again, do not judge me like I'm telling this so I can gain praise. That is not me. I was happy to have been able to produce things for family and friends. At times I would deliver some baby things to a church, and there were always needy mothers there. I was always thankful that they elected to keep their child and not go the easy way out by abortion. Those thoughts were enough to keep me focused and helping where I could.

On the next pages, I have pictures of some of my favorite quilts and afghans. They are in no particular order of making. It was just certain ones carried memories with them. At times people wanted to pay me for certain things. If they argued long enough, I took their money—reluctantly indeed—or a few times someone would order something special and insist that they should have to pay for that. All in all, I had a great and rewarding time. I received so many blessings from God for all the donations!

I have a funny story about two of my quilts. Our nephew Teddy Zahara owns and operates a bar/restaurant in Bathgate, North Dakota. He is my sister Rita's son. He knew, of course, that I made quilts and asked me if I would make one for him. The idea was he would sell chances on it and raffle it off at the bar. He sold all the tickets, and the night of the drawing for the winner, his business picked up nicely. Anyway, I made a little money on the quilt, and he did okay with the increase in customers. All the tickets were sold, and a local woman won it.

The following year, Teddy decided we should do another raffle—same scenario as the year before. The drawing night increased his business again, and everyone was happy. The unbelievable happened as the winner turned out to be the same woman as the previous year. Wow! We couldn't believe it, but that's the "luck of the draw" as they say.

We decided not to proceed with a drawing the following year. We were afraid she might win again, then it really would start looking like some kind of rigged deal. Gosh, in all reality, odds would be astronomically against her winning three in a row!

Quilt making, as many of you might know, starts with cutting squares that are sewn together in beautiful patterns. At one time, in late 1984, I actually cut fifteen thousand squares for quilts I was planning in 1985. There are five quilts in the following pictures where I used many of those squares in early 1985. If I wasn't quilting, I was making afghans or crocheting. I always laugh when I hear people complain about being bored. I usually thought why not take up some of these hobbies, right? I realize this isn't for everyone, and I didn't mean any bad will to those who said that they were bored. On the next pages, please enjoy a small portion of my handiwork.

Many colors and styles of afghans.

MY GOD-GIVEN LIFE

I tried to make all the quilts unique.

Five quilts and four afghans finished from January to March 1985.

Below are some pictures of a few different things that I also made and sold. The top one and lower left is small clowns and dolls that were made to hold potpourri in the bathrooms. One picture, lower right, is dolls for Christmas presents for little girls.

I also began sewing some clothes for kids and some shirts for Aelred. Never had much dust on the sewing machine!

Sometime while we were living in the new house along Highway 1, Aelred and I decided to start making donuts that we would sell. I don't know the reason why, but we did. I always loved the donuts my mother made for us, so the decision was easy as to what recipe we would use. Mother made them the old-fashioned way, which was by using lard and then rendering it to produce the very most flavorful cooking oil. I'm sure this technique started before I was born. On the farms then, most people did their own butchering of animals. The lard was produced during the processing of the fat of the animals. Since we sold the cattle sometime in the mid 1950s, we hadn't been doing any of our own butchering. This left us one option, and that was to buy lard from the locker plant in Langdon.

On the day we made donuts, the first step was to render the lard. Then we would proceed to mix the batter from Mom's recipe. After that, we had the oil that was rendered from the lard, and we used a donut dropper to drop the mix into the oil. At this point, we were only making a few donuts at a time in the oil. Later we had a big-enough pot that we could make eight at once. Aelred mixed the batter, and I dropped and turned the donuts in the oil. We never had a plan in the early days as to how many we were going to make.

We started out by taking them to the farmers market in Langdon. Also attended some craft fairs in and out of town. People told us they loved the donuts. At the same time, we were also making cookies, bars, and even cakes and pies. These were also big sellers at the markets. One year I decided to enter a cooking contest at the Cavalier County Fair in Langdon. It was a contest with a lady known for her baking. Guess what—I won first place. I won a big blue ribbon and bragging rights. *Wow!*

The first-place win brought us new customers. We made donuts for many years. God only knows how many dozen we made. As time progressed, we started gathering quite a following for our bake goods, especially the donuts. Many people would simply come by the house and buy from us. Then more and more of them would call before we cooked and place orders. Some of the orders were huge. We had days where we literally spent all day mixing and making donuts. At some point, lard became harder to find locally, so we started using canola oil. This made it so much quicker to produce donuts on the day's orders. When we first started back in the

1980s, we were charging $1 a dozen. This was quite cheap, and maybe that's why we had so much business. By 2013 we were still making donuts, and the price had increased to $5 a dozen—still very reasonable for the product.

Below I've included a couple of pics taken on a donut cooking day. I remember one day at the farmers market we were selling so many donuts that it looked as if we were going to run out very early, so I stayed and kept selling, and Aelred went home and kept making more and more batches. That may have been one of our best days ever.

October 1985—36 dozen ready for bagging.

MY GOD-GIVEN LIFE

Fall 1991. A smorgasbord of baked goods.

The donut dropper we used for thousands of dozens of donuts over a period of 28 years.

After Aelred quit farming in the late 1970s, he really enjoyed doing wood working. At the new house, he had set up quite a few tools in the basement to build things. He loved doing work with the router. He built all kinds of wood things including doing some baseboard trim. I remember the Christmas of 1988 he decided he was going to build something for all the kids. He decided to put together a mailbox that could be decorated for the Christmas season. They were quite unique, and he was thrilled to be busy with them. Below are some pictures of four of them. The kids were so surprised!

The Christmas mailboxes. December 1988.

I wasn't quite done with projects yet. I was crocheting tablecloths. Here are a few of them, large and small.

I do miss doing these bigger projects.

One of my favorites, made for Joni in January 1986.

Aelred, being nine years older than me, was starting to find work a bit harder. We had a big yard to take care of around the house. So in 1997, we made the decision to sell the house and move into Langdon. It was a small but beautiful house. The house along the highway was sold to the Skjerwheim family from the Nekoma area. As it turned out, their son, Seth, went to the seminary to be a priest. Maybe all the Blessed Virgin Mary artifacts in the house helped him in his journey. There were many statues when we lived there. How happy I was for him.

The house we bought had some stairs going to the basement. This was okay except the laundry room was down there. We were spoiled in the other house as laundry was on the main floor. We grew nervous about going up and down, so we decided to sell this house. We then moved into the Dr. Blanchard house located toward the west side of Langdon. No stairs made it a great place for us. We stayed there quite a few years.

One day I fell in the yard and couldn't get up. It was then we decided to sell that house and move to the new condo, which was right across the church from St. Alphonsus Church. This was really a nice place as no steps to enter, no stairs, and all floor heating including the garage. Also, we could walk across the street to go to Mass. This was all so nice, especially the garage, as we never had any water or ice on the floor after we drove the vehicle into it. The heating bill for the house was so much less because of the heated floors.

Through all these house moves, we continued to stay busy with the many projects. Of course, including the donuts, quilts, and afghans. We were so blessed to have some of the children and their spouses able to help us with all the moving of furnishings. We could never thank them enough. Some furnishings we sold when the move to the small house happened, and then, of course, we had to purchase some things for the next two places. At times it seemed we would never get done moving, but the condo proved to be the last house we lived in!

The years after we quit farming and leading up to 2012 passed so quickly that I won't go into much detail. I was busy with my projects, which you've seen and managed a few trips away from Langdon. The details of some of these are included in part 3. The children came to visit regularly along with all the grandchildren. Life was good.

Rita and I always enjoyed a close relationship.

One of the greatest blessings God bestowed on me was my dear sister Rita. We talked daily on the phone as at that time our telephone plan allowed free long-distance calls. Some of these could last for hours. Now she was not driving anymore, so I was always glad when we could drive to visit her. Above are a couple of pictures of us growing up that show our close relationship over all the years.

The winter of 2011 to 2012 was unbelievable for snow and warmth—little snow—and on March 15, the temperature is sixty-eight degrees. This broke all kinds of records over the state. We were nearly as warm as Dallas,

Texas, where Mary Beth and Jim had recently moved. We missed them along with Melissa, Kristen and Pat, and the great grandkids. Mary Beth and Jim were such good grandparents. I hope the economy will allow them to come back to North Dakota for some visits. By the way, the gas price today is $3.72. I'm sure this hurts many people in a lot of ways.

As I think of more of the children now moving away, I go back to a thought that bothers me. One of the things I was always sorry for is that I never spent enough time with my children—for instance, ball games, wrestling matches, or school plays. I was so afraid that I wouldn't be doing what Grandma Bea would expect. I always felt that she expected everything to be finished. Knowing what I know now, I would not have acted that way today. The children should have come first always. One time when they were smaller, we had a picnic out in the yard. We sat on a blanket and had lunch, fun time, and should have done that more. Trying to be perfect all the time wasn't the best solution for all!

In July 2012, I and my brothers and sisters gathered at Brainard, Minnesota, for a reunion. What a great weekend.

It seemed like we were always being photographed. The cell phones with cameras in them were a great invention. This technology for me, considering my early years living without even running water or electricity, seems unbelievable. The only bad thing about the pictures was no one was posing, so most of the time, I thought I looked terrible—but I suppose those were the thoughts of everyone. I do think some are more photogenic than others, but everyone is humble. Thank God everyone was quite healthy, but problems were beginning to show because of our ages. We all agreed our families had grown, but we thanked God that nobody had cognitive disabilities. We had only lost one child in the family with the passing of Rita's oldest son, Edward. Thank you, God!

2012 also brought more sadness as God called some of the family home. We lost two of Aelred's sisters, Joan and Ellen. They were like sisters to me, and I always enjoyed their visits. Ellen had a trip planned to visit the farm this year, but God had other plans. We also lost Ellen's husband, Ed, and her oldest son, Cress—really sad year.

My arms had been giving me trouble. It was hard to lift as they felt they weighed a ton. Eventually they got a bit better, and I was able to go back to making donuts. I needed to satisfy our many customers, the farmers market was calling also, and I was able to continue to provide them. Again, the price was $5 a dozen. There weren't many people who wanted to make them, thus I could have charged more but didn't. I was just hoping someone would carry on the service after I quit.

Lately my weak arms, neurotherapy, and fibromyalgia have been my cross. Maybe if God hadn't sent me these, I wouldn't have offered anything to him. It seems at times we don't think of God when things are great. Therefore, the crosses He gives us to bear allows us to offer up our prayers and daily works to Him.

I watch the Fox news channel daily and read some newspapers occasionally. I try to keep up a bit on world happenings. One day I read that Ireland may soon be legalizing abortion. My God, they will join the rest of the world with a law to take any life. God save us all! So many states are now legalizing same-sex marriage. I wonder how the world can continue into the future. They are killing babies, which is leaving many couples childless. I don't think the world can continue without babies.

I learned that Mary Beth and Jim had decided not to go to Florida and were returning to North Dakota. God answered my prayers. We also had made a trip to Arizona to see Kevin and Becky—very enjoyable and not sure how many more of these trips we could do. Aelred loved sitting outside for hours in the warm sun. His legs have been giving him trouble. He gets blisters and twitchy legs. I was afraid there was more wrong with him as he labored with breathing and lost a lot of weight. I just couldn't bear to see him sick and maybe gone from this earth. I wanted to believe that whatever happens would be God's will and tried my best to comply with his wishes.

The early spring and summer of 2013 were so different with so much rain. Most farmers had a tough time getting the crops planted. Steven only got half. I decided to postpone my shoulder surgery until fall and then could be laid up during the winter. I also had hurt my back in January and was waiting to find a fix for that. My hobbies of quilting and crocheting were pretty much nonexistent lately.

I enjoyed our short trips during the last year that Aelred and I took to the Devil's Lake casino. He loved the food there, and I liked playing with the penny machines and all the noise the machines made—not high class but sometimes made enough for a child's pair of shoes. I played a couple of favorite machines that gave me some ca-ching! I always loved these trips. We started by praying the Rosary and the Chaplet of the Holy Cross every time we went somewhere. Seems like that made us enjoy each other's company more. Of course, we always prayed for a safe trip.

As I listen to Fox news again, I learned they are looking into four scandals perpetrated by the democrats. I can't believe what is happening to this country. Are there any honest people remaining anymore?

The crop that got planted was looking beautiful. Aelred seemed to watch this crop growing more than he had paid attention in previous years. He also took a great interest in the new Cenex/Harvest States elevator being built. Langdon was also celebrating its 125-year anniversary as a town. Margie Garske, Aelred's cousin on the Dettler side, came with her daughter and her husband for a visit. She was always good looking and had fun growing up in Langdon. Her family was aways playing tricks on someone in the family. This would probably be her last visit to where she would remember us as her age has produced some dementia. In July, Steven and Barb hosted a family day at the farm. It was so nice of them to have everyone there to celebrate Aelred's eighty-eighth birthday, my seventy-ninth birthday, and the one hundredth birthday of the farm.

Around the time of the family day, Aelred was having really bad leg problems. The least little bump he would get a blister, and it would leak water. It was a real chore keeping him dry as his legs were almost running continually with water. This continued into late summer and early fall. Obviously, like I wrote earlier, he had more problems than he told me.

On the morning of October 17, 2013, I awoke to find him on the floor on his stomach. He was unable to move, and the ambulance came and took him to the hospital in Langdon. The doctors worked to get him awake, and after some testing, they let him know his kidneys were failing. They offered to start dialysis, but he said he didn't want to live a life that had no quality to it. I can't imagine the courage it took for him to make this decision. Evidently, he had been giving it much thought before this day. His father had also died from kidney failure in 1950.

In the hospital, he was given the last rites and confession. I was relieved that he was able to receive the Sacraments. Many people are less fortunate and die without confessing their sins. Of course, Aelred was a sinner as we all are. The later years of his life were filled with constant praying of the Rosary. He also spent many hours at the church for adoration of the Blessed Eucharist to ask the Lord for forgiveness for being a sinner. He genuinely prayed to be forgiven for any sins committed against myself and the children. Yes, the Lord can truly be a savior if you will just ask for forgiveness.

All the kids, along with the grandkids, were called to the hospital. He had so many visitors during the afternoon, and he recognized everyone. I think he was curious why everyone was there as it wasn't sinking in how bad his health was. He actually ate his supper (of course this reminded us of our saying that "he would never miss a meal"). He also prayed parts of the Rosary with us. Around 8:00 p.m., his kidneys started to fail, and he was given pain reliever. He seemed very agitated for the next few hours and tried to get out of bed a few times. He passed away peacefully early the following morning while Kevin was holding his hand.

He would be the third one to die in my family as my brother Melvin and his wife Sharon were also gone. I was in shock with Aelred's fast death. It is interesting to note here that he got his final wish, which was as follows: Many, many, times he told me that he was so afraid to have to be put in the nursing home. For whatever reason, that seemed like a death sentence for him, yet he was strong enough to refuse the dialysis.

The wake brought so many people, who were both friends and family. He had been preceded in death by his only brother, Gerald, and two of his sisters, Joan and Ellen. The remaining survivor of the five Dettler children born to Leonard and Beatrice is Moria, who is still alive and doing well today in Dayton, Ohio.

The funeral filled the church with many nephews and nieces traveling quite some distance to attend. The children and many grandchildren were also present. Aelred had been the Grand Knight of the Knights of Columbus for Chapter 5057 in Langdon, so the knights were dressed in formal dress including their swords. They marched in as a group and sat on guard during the Mass. Burial was in the Catholic cemetery in Langdon next to his parents.

A number of years back, Aelred and I decided to give a year of our life for service to the church. We thought we needed to give back to the Lord for His blessings and to atone for our past sins. I served as the president of the local chapter of the Catholic Daughters of America, or CDA. Some of our work included, among other activities, doing what we could to keep the Catholic grade school up and running. Aelred, as mentioned above, served as the president of the Knights of Columbus, or KCs. This organization does many things such as raising money for the church to even education. Needless to say, we were busy but felt fulfilled in our efforts. One of the highlights included winning first place in the scrapbook competition. This is a contest among all the KC chapters in the entire state of North Dakota. It was indeed quite an honor.

My broken hip started a time of aging for me. It turned into a very hard sentence. All the pain was offered to God. Next came the operation to take the metal from the hip surgery, then there was no walking. After many months and many tests, there was still a cracked hip. A new hip was put in again and five days in the hospital and four weeks of therapy. My time now is spent at the sewing machine, and I thank God I can do those projects as the time would be extra long as I can't go out anymore.

I am still struggling with the hip replacement. I just don't seem to be able to walk alone. I now have a buggy which I need to hang onto. One leg is now one-half inch shorter, which is some of the problem. Things are so much harder when one is limited. It seems I should be better even though I'm eighty-one-and-a-half years old, but they really are.

God has been good to me lately. I've had so many people stop by to visit. It's always nice to see and hear from everyone and know they are doing God's work and using God's hands by visiting the elderly. This week has been a time of additional praying. Rita is in the hospital in Grand Forks. My brother Jerry is having surgery on his back. Then there is my friend Jean's funeral. My grandson Derek is having hip surgery at the Mayo Clinic. My cousin John Koropatnicki died suddenly. So many young people today with health issues.

The hardest part of the week was Mary Beth's surgery and the news that she had cancer. I am devastated. She just got to a point in life to retire from her dental work career and will now have to fight. God will be with her as she is and has been a true servant of the Lord. She has lived her life as a devout Catholic, and she has done so much to help people. I will be praying for a miracle for her.

The months of Jan to April 2017 I spent in Phoenix at Kevin and Becky's—beautiful as usual. I went last year for a month. Mary Beth continued to fight her cancer. She found a doctor in the Phoenix area to help her on her journey of homeopathic medicine to help with her cancer treatments. After she came to Arizona, I made the decision to purchase a house so that Mary Beth and Jim could live with me. She had been wanting to move there for some time, and this would help. Kevin was such a help getting us a great deal on a beautiful home located in Queen Creek close to his and Becky's house. They moved in with me about March 1st. She was so excited, but God had a different plan. She was coughing so bad day and night. I hated to see her suffering and wished I could take some of her pain. I left to go home in April. She went so fast after I left there, but her family was able to be there for those last days of her life.

My beautiful house in Queen Creek, AZ.

She passed away April 29, 2017. I was so sad, but I couldn't cry as I knew she was prepared to die. She had prepared her whole life for that moment. I knew in my heart that she would certainly be in heaven. I missed her terribly. Her wake and funeral were held back in Grand Forks. Those two days I hardly knew what went on—so much hurt. I pray I never have to go through this again with one of my children.

Mary Beth and her ever-present smile.

I thought I would be living in my beautiful home with her and Jim. Kevin and St. Joseph helped me sell the house for a profit. Jim then left to return to Minnesota. Her death was so hard on him. We were also saddened to know that Mary Beth's first social security check came and had to be returned. She never even got a chance at retirement. So many things in life don't seem fair, but our faith tells us that God's plan is better. So now I will be going to Kevin and Becky's this winter, which is still great, just not my own home.

We had another family reunion in June. It was in Grand Forks. We had so many laughs over the photo albums Mom had made for each of us. These albums will be a thing of the past, as I said earlier, because of cell phones. I thank God for the great relationships we enjoy between my brothers and sisters, no grudges, and have been able to forgive when there were offenses. Visiting with my family continually brought thoughts of Mary Beth. I was missing her so much, but I wouldn't wish her back with all the suffering she endured at the end. I did get a call while we were there form Aelred's sister Moira. Her oldest son had passed away. He had died as his father had at home—with a heart attack.

I don't mean for my story to contain so many sad moments now, but the time is coming for all of us to go to our heavenly home. Pray that we can always be prepared through our prayers and actions for the journey to heaven. It was nice to hear from the grandchildren this fall. With some of them close and some quite far away and with busy lives, their visits are always held dear. I've always regretted that I'm not the greatest phone person as I don't call as I should, but I would love to have their calls. Plan to get to Arizona if all my health problems can be handled. I do know the weather there is better for my muscles, but who knows. This fall Steven paid off the land he bought from us. I do pray that the land will stay in the Dettler family. Six generations is quite a feat in over one hundred years. It is really cool that the same house is still there.

I am sad this year (2017) at Christmas. This will be my first time in eighty-three years that I was not at Christmas Mass due to illness. I was able to watch two Masses on my favorite TV channel, EWTN, but wasn't able to receive Communion but received a spiritual Communion. Jesus came to my soul in this fashion. The sadness is amplified as I didn't hear from Mary Beth. Also, it's been four Christmases since Aelred has been gone.

The time since I returned from AZ has flown by. I had left my two angels (Kevin and Becky) in AZ and returned home to my angels here in Langdon, namely Chalmer, Min, and my close friends. If not for them, I would not be able to be at home, which I cherish at my age. I also have a few more angels that bring Holy Communion on Fridays. That is a great boost every week.

After Mary Beth's death, Min Gette, who belonged to our pray group, started stopping by the house to visit and check on me. She came every day after her work. What a blessing as she would ask for how she could help me. Sometimes I would have her bring a few groceries. Sometimes she would help clean the house. I could not have stayed in my home alone if it wasn't for Min. I met and loved her children. She spends time visiting and helping others that are sick or homebound. What a saint.

I lost my sister Rita this year. How I miss her also. As I said earlier, we talked almost daily. She could pour her heart out and I would to her. I loved driving to her home, picking her up, and going to Cavalier to the secondhand store or Grafton for chicken at Shenanigans. Her son Jimmy calls me often as I'm sure he misses talking with his mother. He lives in

Nashville now, but he used to be a server at a restaurant in Cavalier that Rita and I would visit. It was one of our favorite places also. I always enjoy Jimmy's calls. He sends me licorice at Christmas every year.

Grand Forks reunion after Rita's passing.

Thanks to Mary Beth's family, who come to visit when they can. They and their kids are so precious. I hope some of my prayers will help them through life as they get by without their mom. Thank God for the family that stays in touch. I get to see many of the kids and grandkids on what is called Nix Play. This was a Christmas present from Kevin and Becky.

Pictures can be sent anytime and anywhere, so I can see pictures of all who send me pics.

I am so thankful for all that Chalmer does for me. He does so much including all my paperwork, insurance issues, and banking. He is always kind and never once has he ever been harsh to me. God bless him. I am also so happy when he brings his grandkids to visit. They are also so precious. Thank you to David also as he calls me every week, usually on Sundays. He also has tried to come visit even though he lives so far away.

My greatest day of the week now is Wednesdays. We go to Mass, and then all go for coffee. How special is this closeness, and I know I can call them anytime if I feel the need to talk. I know they will pray for me and I will them if needed.

My brother Ronald has been so close to me over the years, much like Rita. His wife, Rosanna, passed away in November 2017. Since that time, we have spent a lot of time together. We go to Mass often and out for meals either in Langdon or Devil's Lake. He especially has been a Godsend after I was not able to drive anymore. He also has spent his entire life preparing for life with God in heaven after death. I've always been proud of how he lived his life and how he taught his children and grandchildren the fruits of a holy life. I was shocked when I learned of his cancer. When he was diagnosed, he didn't complain or be in a bad mood. He is such a champion for the Lord. He passed away in the summer of 2022.

In December I was at home and went to take some clothes from the dryer. Something in my back snapped—ended up in the hospital with terrible pain. I was sent to the Grand Forks and had a vertebrae cemented together. I spent a little more time in the hospital and knew then that my days of staying home alone were over. That was the moment I decided to come to the Osnabrock Living Center—this is how this book started—a great place, and the help is so good. Min comes to visit every week.

I don't know what I would have done without Chalmer and Lori as they got the condo ready for a sale. Lori cleaned it all and organized to get rid of all the furnishings. Becky and her sister Kathy organized and had a rummage sale to get rid of the many boxes of items left after the big furniture was gone. Next Chalmer and Lori decorated my room at the home with my furnishings. I now have exactly what I need. There are some things I wish I could have kept, but I'm okay—God had the plan, and I listened.

My back healed enough aided by some extra doctoring, which allowed me to travel, so I spent some of the winter in Arizona in January 2022 and 2023. During this time, Chalmer was working to get the condo sold. He decided to try to sell it privately to save the cost of the realtor. He started out asking for around $200,000. The cost when new was $145,000. That was a number of years ago and prices of homes had almost doubled.

This project proved to be very time-consuming for him. He did have a few people interested before he put it up for sale. He did showings for those folks but couldn't get much interest generated. He liked to show on the weekends so as to not interfere with running the bank. It seemed hard to get folks to look then. He did try so hard and spent so much time on the project. The other kids thought he should list it to free up his time again, but he decided he would lower the price to $175,000. This was helpful and he got some more people to look. After a couple of showings, there was a retired couple that loved the location across from St. Alphonsus. They negotiated a price a bit lower but did decide to buy it. I was so happy, and I know Chalmer was more thrilled. It had taken almost a year and half to sell it. I was sad to see it go. I guess it was our home for a good time and the last time I would own home.

Our Condo across the street from St. Alphonsus.

In 2024 I went to Kevin and Becky's again and stayed about seven weeks. During the mid part of February, my brothers and sisters came to Phoenix for another reunion. We spent almost a week visiting and reminiscing—lots more fun. Before they left for their homes, they all showed up and surprised me with a party to celebrate my ninetieth birthday, which was coming up on June 21st. I was so happy for two reasons—the fact they thought of me and the fact that I've made it to be ninety. The picture below is taken at Kevin and Becky's at the celebration.

My 90th birthday celebration in Arizona, 2024.

**In the picture right behind me, left to right: Kevin, Becky, Connie, Diane, Corriene, Dennis;
next row: Lorna, Annette, Colleen;
back row: Louis, Jerry, Larry.**

That was our first reunion since Ronald's passing. He, along with Rita and Melvin, is truly missed.

The following is a poem that my brother Jerry wrote for me and shared at the birthday party.

Dear Doreen,

There are a couple things that are older than you, I just can't think what they are at the moment. You are 32,000 days old, 90 trips around the sun, and there have been 15 US presidents during your lifetime. Not that I was counting. LOL

You wake up some days. Your back gives you grief, tired hips, some aches and a set of false teeth. But through all of this and through the aches and pain, to all of us, you're still exactly the same. So, although you may feel older and at times a bit sore, we've loved you through all the years and we'll continue to love you for more.

Happy 90th birthday young lady with a grin and don't forget to put your teeth in. Oh, and one more thing: Just to up the ante, when you're feeling down, put on your big girl panties!

This page is a great way to leave part 2 of the book now. I'm ready for the big girl panties! What a precious ninetieth celebration. I have an unbelievable family.

Part 3

My God-Given Life

I am and always will be a devout Catholic. Part 3 of the book here is the story of my incredible faith in God. There will be a few things in chronological order and then some stories in no particular order. I have some prayers that I pray. There are some pages of education that will help the reader understand my deep adoration of the Blessed Virgin Mary. There are some pages devoted to four very important trips that continued to strengthen my faith. Some of the pages will deal with the plan God has for my life here on earth. There are some random thoughts that may guide the reader to their own increase of faith. I have a section on personal apparitions. I have some personal prayers that some may enjoy seeing.

Before I was even six years old, I already had an incredible love for God. This was bolstered by some special people in my life. Of course, Mom and Daddy provided perfect examples of Catholicism for me. Daddy would kneel on the bare floor as the nightly Rosary was said. He and Mom always encouraged my love for God and to pray often.

Uncle Charlie, as you learned, lived with us in the early years, and he also set a great example to follow, but I have to say two people that were truly inspirational were Grandma Carignan (Daddy's mother) and Grandma Fritz (Mom's mother). I spent quite a bit of time staying overnight with them. With Grandma Carignan, we went to Mass every day. I loved it. She was so devoted to praying, and I loved her petunias. Grandma Carignan also spent some time staying with us during the winter months, so again I had a chance to learn from her. I didn't spend as much time with Grandma Fritz, but she was still so influential.

I remember Grandma Fritz praying. She would go to the crucifix, stand there, make three signs of the cross, say a short prayer, and finish with three more signs of the cross—truly inspired me! You could tell she was sincere about prayers. I realize this all sounds odd for a little girl, but it is absolutely true.

First Communion

When it came time for my first Communion, I was more than ready. I knew the answers to the questions asked by the nuns. I was so excited. First Communion was on Sunday, but we had our first confession first. I wore a lovely white dress, white shoes, and matching veil. I am sure Rita also wore it a few years later.

First Communion day.

The first Communion group in 1940.

The Catholic church in Leroy was the site of the first Communion. Of course, I had been there many times previously—a beautiful old church.

During the summers, we had a religion class at the church again in Bathgate. The nuns taught us over a period of two weeks. Many of the kids weren't so excited about it, but I was eager to learn more. Some of the idea for more catechism was to help prepare us for upcoming confirmation.

A very large confirmation group.

I learned new prayers during our summer school. When it came time for confirmation, it was just like the first Communion—I was ready. I was praying the Rosary often and adding new prayers at the same time. Usually at confirmation we chose saints' names, and I chose St. Theresa, so now my official name is Cecilia Doreen Theresa Carignan. I have over the years prayed many prayers to St. Theresa for intercession. She helped.

Rita and I at confirmation with our sponsors.

The confirmation was held in Cavalier as we were living close to there at the time. I literally could feel the Holy Spirit flood me with grace as the bishop prayed over me. He said, "Come, Holy Spirit." God was with me that day. I didn't hear from any of the others that may have had the same experience. I had. All I can say is that it was a wonderful feeling of love! I do also remember at my first Communion the same feeling as I received the body and blood of Christ. Then some years later, I had the same feelings. While Father Rudd was in Langdon at St. Alphonsus, I and Mary Bisenius were given the privilege to distribute Communion to the shut-ins and the hospital patients. This is one of the best jobs of my life. So now I have received four of the seven precious sacraments from the Catholic Church. The four are baptism, confession, communion, and confirmation. Of course, then marriage would bring the number to five. I would hope that at the time of death, I will have the sixth sacrament administered, which is the last rites. The last sacrament which I can't receive is holy orders, or priesthood.

The Rosary

The Rosary has been my favorite prayer since I was old enough to pray it. I watched and learned from Mom and

Daddy. As stated earlier, all my relatives were Catholic, so I was comfortable praying this way. There have been very few days of my life that I have missed saying at least one Rosary. I find it easy to talk to the Blessed Virgin Mary when I am praying to her. The following is a list of what is called the "Fifteen Promises of Mary Most Holy to Those Who Pray the Rosary." These are not the only reasons I pray the Rosary, but they make sense.

1. Whoever shall faithfully serve me by the recitation of the Rosary shall receive signal graces.
2. I promise my special protection and the greatest graces to all those who recite the Rosary.
3. The Rosary shall be a powerful armor against hell. It will destroy vice, decrease sin, and defeat heresy.
4. It will cause virtue and good works to flourish; it will obtain for souls and abundant mercy of God; it will withdraw the hearts of men from the love of the world and its vanities and will lift them to the desire of eternal things. Oh, that souls would sanctify themselves by this means.
5. The soul that recommends itself to me by the recitation of the Rosary shall not perish.

6. Whoever shall recite the Rosary devoutly, applying himself to the consideration of its sacred mysteries, shall never be conquered by misfortune: if he be a sinner, he shall not perish by an unprovided death; if he be just, he shall remain in the grace of God. He shall become worthy of eternal life.
7. Whoever shall have a true devotion for the Rosary shall not die without the sacraments of the church.
8. Those who are faithful to the recitation of the Rosary shall have, during their life and at death, the light of God and the plenitude of His graces. At the moment of death, they shall participate in the merits of the saints in paradise.
9. I shall deliver from purgatory those who have been devoted to the Rosary.
10. The faithful children of the Rosary shall merit a high degree of glory in heaven.
11. You shall obtain all you ask of me by the recitation of the Rosary.
12. All those who propagate the Holy Rosary shall be aided by me in their necessities.
13. I have obtained from my Divine son that all the advocates of the Rosary shall have for intercessors

the entire celestial court during their life and at the hour of their death.

14. All who recite the Rosary are my sons and daughters of My son, Jesus Christ.
15. Devotion to my Rosary is a great sign of predestination.

These are some powerful words! They have been the guidance I have used my entire life. It's all here for the taking—a life without strife, a plan to provide you a perfect life after death immediately without fear of purgatory. There are so many graces you receive to help make God-loving decisions in your everyday life. Our blessed Mother couldn't offer any more kindness from her and Jesus for the tiny asking of a daily fifteen-minute prayer. I hope this gives you the sense of why I pray the Rosary every day. I'm asked daily why I always have such a beautiful smile every day. Well, why would I not smile as the Blessed Mother blesses me every day. I especially like the idea promised in number 6. It says whoever prays with devotion "will never be conquered by misfortune." Do you remember the story from 1978 when the wheat crop was destroyed by hail? The Rosary was our salvation, and we were not conquered. It's easy for me to believe number 15—to me life is indeed predetermined by praying the Rosary. I have said many times here that the only goal you should have in life is saving your soul for heaven.

Whoever shall have a true devotion for the rosary shall not die without the sacraments of the Church.

The Blessed Mary and Jesus with rosary.

God has blessed me my entire life. Has it been a perfect life? No. Has it been a time of no sin? No. Have I done all I could to be a witness to my faith? No. Yes, I prayed my Rosary daily, rarely if ever missed Mass, went to confession often, volunteered my time with Catholic organizations, including a year as president of the Catholic Daughters, distribute Communion to the shut-ins, worked with Mary Bisenius and the altar society, and was a humble servant to the Lord—but I felt I needed to do more. I already was deeply devoted to the Blessed Virgin Mary, and when I prayed to her, I seemed to hear her calling me. If I was to be a stronger witness for the love of God, I needed to visit the places that our Lady was appearing. She was telling her followers what was needed for our soul to attain eternity in heaven. I was yearning for an even closer relationship with Our Lady.

So I set about a plan to visit Fatima. That was such a moving experience. After returning from there, I had a call to go to Lourdes and then to Medjugorje (twice). I know you may think these trips for just excuses to visit somewhere, and maybe, to a small extent, this is true, but I was going for Our Lady. The following stories are of those trips. There is quite a bit of material I've included for you to analyze. Please bear with me as it may seem long but worth it!

Fatima

I traveled with a group of parishioners from St. Alphonsus and a few other parishes when I made my pilgrimage to Fatima. I had no idea I would ever make this trip either because of funding or health issues, but I made it and was so glad I did.

Fatima is a small town located in central Portugal about forty-five miles northwest of Lisbon. It is home to the Sanctuary of Fatima, a Catholic pilgrimage site. A short version of the history that some do not know goes like this.

During World War I, Pope Benedict XV made repeated pleas for peace. Finally, in May 1917, he made a direct appeal to the Blessed Mother to intercede for peace in the world. Just a week later, Our Lady began to appear in Fatima to three shepherd children. On May 13, the children saw two quick flashes of light, much like lightning, even though the sky was totally clear. Then they looked up and saw "a lady, clothed in white, brighter than the sun, radiating a light clearer and more intense than a crystal cup filled with sparkling water lit by burning sunlight." This was the description later quoted from Lucia dos Santos, one of the three. She said, "Do not be afraid. I will not harm you as I come from heaven." She asked them to come to this place at the same hour on the thirteenth for six months. All three agreed when asked if they were willing to offer themselves to God and bear all the sufferings. She said, "Then you are going to have much to suffer, but the grace of God will be your comfort."

They fell to the ground and prayed this prayer communicated to them:

> O most Holy Trinity, I adore Thee; my God my God,
> I love thee in the most blessed sacrament.

This became the Eucharist prayer. The Lady then said, "Say the Rosary every day to bring peace to the world and the end of the war." She then began to rise and move toward the east and disappeared.

The word spread, and each month, on the thirteenth, the flash of light occurred, and then the apparition of Mary appeared. On this visit, she gave the children this prayer to pray after each decade of the Rosary. This is still prayed today:

> O my Jesus, forgive us our sins, save us from the fires of hell. Lead all souls to heaven especially those in most need of your mercy.

It is an amazing story which you can read in much more detail on the internet, but there are two remaining parts I will relate here. Our Lady gave the children three secrets which they held until the time they were told to release them. I have them listed after the next paragraph.

The greatest miracle to occur since Christ's resurrection is the miracle that was predicted here as to date, time of day, and location. This is known as "the Miracle of the Sun." On October 13, 1917, just as Our Lady predicted, the sun whirled and zig-zagged, casting colors about the crowd as it began to descend toward the earth. The seventy thousand assembled people cried out in terror. Some people saw the miracle from fifteen to twenty-five miles away. Many blind people were healed, cripples were healed suddenly, public confession of sins, and commitments of conversion to the religious life. Scientists around the world could not explain the phenomena. Doubters and skeptics became believers.

To reduce space, I have only given you the abbreviated story. I have been a believer and took this trip to see firsthand the location and to pray to the Blessed Virgin as the children and their followers had done. Here are the three secrets as told by the children.

Secret 1: Vision of hell

Our Lady showed us a great sea of fire which seemed to be under the earth. Plunged in this fire were demons and souls in human form, like transparent burning embers, all blackened or burnished bronze, floating about in the configuration, now raised into the air by the flames that issued from within themselves together with great clouds of smoke, now falling back on every side like sparks in a huge fire, without weight or equilibrium, and amid shrieks and groans of pain and despair, which horrified us and made us tremble with fear. The demons could be distinguished by their terrifying and repulsive likeness to frightful and unknown animals, all black and transparent, this vision lasted bur an instant. Our Lady then spoke and explained that devotion to the Immaculate Heart of Mary was a means to save souls from going to hell. You have seen where the poor souls of sinners go. To save and establish in the world devotion to my immaculate heart. This will save many souls, and there will be peace.

Secret 2: World War I and II

The war will end, but if people do not cease offending God, a worse one will break out during the Pontificate of Pius XI. When you see a night illuminated by an unknown light, know that this is a great sign given you by God that He is about to punish the world for its crimes by means of war, famine, and persecutions of the church and of the Holy Father. To prevent this, I shall come to ask for the consecration of Russia to my immaculate heart and the Communion of reparation on the first Saturdays.

Our Lady spoke of the errors of Russia, which many believe refers to communism. She says, "If my requests are heeded, Russia will be converted, and there will be peace; if not, she will spread her errors throughout the world, causing wars and persecutions of the church. The good will be martyred; the Holy Father will have much to suffer; various nations will be annihilated. In the end, my immaculate heart will triumph. The Holy Father will consecrate Russia to me, and she will be converted, and a period of peace will be granted."

Secret 3: Penance and Papal assignation attempt

This secret contains much apocalyptic imagery including a vision of a pope who is shot. Pope John Paul believed this vision had much to do with his own experience though the Virgin Mary never mentions it specially. According to the interpretation of the "little shepherds," which was also confirmed recently by Sister Lucia (one of the three children who received these secrets), "the bishop clothed in white" who prays for all the faithful is the pope. As he makes his way with great difficulty toward the cross amid the corpses of those who were martyred, he falls to the ground, apparently dead, under the hail of gunfire.

After the assassination attempt of the Pope on May 13, 1981, it appeared evident that it was a "mother's hand that guided the bullet's path," enabling "the Pope in his throes" to halt "at the threshold of death."

Another large part of this third vision is penance, calling the world to come back to God. At the left of Our Lady and a little above, we saw an angel with a flaming sword in his left hand; flashing, it gave out flames that looked as though they would set the world on fire, but they died out in contact with the splendor that Our Lady radiated toward him with her fight hand: pointing to the earth with his right hand, the angel cried out in a loud voice: "Penance, penance, penance!"

As with the story of the Rosary, these again are some powerful words. The main goal for us to understand is that we need to pray the Rosary for world peace and do penance for our sins. To me it seems, with all the troubles in the world, that we are failing in fulfilling the wishes that Our Lady asked for at Fatima. Is my faith telling me that we may be close to some kind of reprimand from our God? I pray that our world can turn back to the Lord.

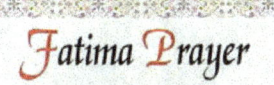

Fatima Basilica was built to honor Our Lady.

These three received the visions of Our Lady.

The 70,000 who witnessed "the Miracle of the Sun"

Our Lady of Fatima.

Since my return from Fatima, I experienced a wonderful feeling of Our Lady's love and healing powers available. Over the years, there have been many documented miracles. That fact keeps the disbelievers at bay. Before I talk about my trip to Lourdes, I want to share the following thoughts with you. I want to be an even better witness of the Catholic faith. I wrote this to remind us of our commitment to God through our faith.

Dear Children of God,

All of you have come into the Catholic faith when you received baptism. This removed the original sin from your soul. I became Catholic because of my parents' wish that I would always receive the graces of God through my faith. For you, it was our desire that faith would grow as you made your first confession. This allowed you to tell your sins to the priest and receive absolute forgiveness and do our penance. (No joke, we can't tell God those sins and be forgiven).
The priest, acting in the body of Christ, absolves you from them. Graces and the love of God are given to you. Then the Sacrament of Confirmation turns you into soldiers of Christ. We are all sinners, of which I may be the greatest, and need the Sacrament of Healing of Confession. You must confess

sins at Eastertime every year or suffer the pain of sin. The Sacrament of the Eucharist, God's body and blood are truly present, and we learned unless we eat the body and drink the blood, there will be no life within you. That means no grace either to keep you from committing sins, especially mortal sin, which destroys our souls. When you receive the sacrament on marriage, a promise is made to raise kids in the Catholic faith. Then in old age or sickness, you receive the Sacrament of Last Rites. When dying, the body gives up the soul alone to God—will our souls be ready to meet God for a life of happiness or a life of eternal fire due to mortal sin?—and at this point, nothing can be changed!

Lourdes

I went to Lourdes with another group of Catholic parishioners. We got a bit of history from the priest that organized the trip, arriving in France and then a bus ride to Lourdes, which is a small town in southwestern France in the foothills of the Pyrenees mountains. According to our guide, in 1858, a fourteen-year-old peasant named Bernadette Soubirous proclaimed she had eighteen encounters with the Virgin Mary. This has made the area one of the most visited sites by Catholics in the world. At the sixteenth appearance,

Bernadette questioned the apparition as to who she was and was told that she was Mary, the mother of Jesus, calling herself the Immaculate Conception. The spiritual message is that of personal conversion. Our Lady tells Bernadette that the important thing to gain happiness in the next life—you must accept the cross in this life. Our Lady instructed Bernadette to dig in the ground next to the grotto where she was appearing. A spring miraculously appeared where there had been no water. It turned out to have water flowing with healing powers and is active to this day. Many people have bathed in the water and filled bottles from the spring to take healing powers home. Some people come on pilgrimage in search of strength and guidance in times of distress and difficulty. For many sick pilgrims, Lourdes gives an opportunity to bathe in the healing waters of the spring and to find peace with their prognosis rather than to seek a miraculous cure. To date, the Catholic Church has recognized seventy miracles resulting from the intervention of God with intercession of Our Lady of Lourdes. The last miracle was declared in 2013. It involved an Italian lady suffering severe high blood pressure and many other problems, who visited Lourdes in 1989. She was cured. Please keep in mind that the Catholic Church does exhaustive research before announcing a miracle.

Our Lady asked Bernadette to tell the priests more than one time to have a chapel built. Eventually it was built. Now there is an entire complex built to honor Our Lady of Lourdes. There are several religious buildings and monuments around the original grotto. There are three basilicas—the Basilica of Our Lady of the Immaculate Conception, Rosary Basilica, and Basilica of St. Pius X. These sites are visited by millions every year.

This is a short story of an unbelievable place. It is impossible to grasp the flowing spring until a personal visit is made. The presence of the Our Lady of the Immaculate Conception is felt everywhere. It's indescribable!

The following is for the nonbelievers. At the conclusion of the eighteen visions, Bernadette joined the Sisters of Charity at the age of twenty-two. She disliked the attention that she received because of the visions and lived the simple life of a consecrated religious until she died of tuberculosis at age thirty-five in 1879. She was buried at the chapel of St. Joseph in Nevers, France. In 1909, thirty years later, her body was exhumed as part of the usual requirements for saint hood. As the coffin was opened in front of many witnesses, including the Bishop of Nevers, the mayor of the town, his principal deputy, several cannons, and the nuns who originally put her in the coffin, they found the body of Bernadette in a perfect state of preservation. There was not the slightest trace of an unpleasant smell. So rigid was the perfect body that it was able to be rolled and washed.

Then again, in 1919, an identification of the body was again necessary for the purpose of beautification and canonization (sainthood). Another euhemerization was done, and again the body was in perfect condition. Finally, in 1925, forty-six years after her death, Bernadette was proclaimed blessed and a saint. Her body was placed on display in the chapel of Saint-Girard, where it can be seen today.

The Miraculous Spring at Lourdes.

The Basilica at Lourdes, France, and Our Lady's Grotto.

Here is the Prayer to Our Lady of Lourdes.

O glorious Mother of God, so powerful under your special title of Our Lady of Lourdes, to you we raise our hearts and hands to implore your powerful intercession in obtaining from the gracious heart of Jesus all the helps and graces necessary for our spiritual and temporal welfare and for the special favor we so earnestly seek. Our Lady of Lourdes, pray for us. Saint Bernadette, pray for us. *Amen.*

Saint Bernadette.

Medjugorje

I am so excited about this trip. Of course, I am happy to be going overseas again and hoping to see the apparition of Our Lady, but this trip will be really special. The reason: Mary Beth and my sister Rita are going to accompany me. So far, as you've seen, I didn't go with any close family when I traveled to Fatima and Lourdes. This will make the time go so fast as we have so much to talk about. You've learned earlier in my writings about the deep Catholic conviction Mary Beth had her entire life. I have not written much about Rita, but she also has a tremendous deep Catholic faith and adores the Blessed Virgin Mary, much as I do. So, with two angels traveling with me, I will feel so safe as we visit a new country.

Prior to 1981, Medjugorje (which in Croatian means "between the mountains") was just a tiny farming village located in a harsh and desolate corner of the former Yugoslavia. On June 24, 1981, for the first time, Our Lady appeared to a group of local kids. This would be the first of a long series that continues to this day. Her appearance was to deliver to the world a message of peace and conversions through prayer and fasting. On this day, the kids were walking on Mount Crnica (today called the Apparition Hill), and they saw in the sky a evanescent figure of a beautiful woman holding a child in her arms. They recognized her as the Virgin Mary, but she didn't speak and made a sign for them to approach her, but they were scared and ran away. At home, they told their parents what happened, but the adults, frightened by the possible consequences (don't forget that the Socialist Federal Republic of Yugoslavia was officially atheist) told them to shut up.

The news, however, is so resounding that it spreads quickly in the village; and the following day, a group of curious gather in the same place and at the same time in the hope of a new apparition, which happens right away. This time the group of six has changed out a couple of people but still numbers six that appear to have been chosen by Our Lady, and they watch as the Madonna appears on a cloud without the child but bright and beautiful. This time the six run fast among the rocks, brambles, and weeds toward the top of the mountain. There is no trail, but they never got a scratch and tell they felt transported by a mysterious force. Dressed beautifully matching her loving blue eyes and twelve stars around her head, she has few words with the youngsters. She prays with them and promises to come back.

The third day, one thousand people gather, attracted by a bright glow. Vicki, one of the six, on the advice of the elders, throws a bottle of holy water on the appreciation to verify if the figure is a celestial or demonic entity. "If you are Madonna, stay with us. If you are not, go away." Our Lady smiles, and when she is asked "what's your name?" for the first time, she says, "I am the Blessed Virgin Mary." She repeats the word *peace* several times, and when the apparition is over and the visionaries leave the hill, Our Lady appears only to Marija. She is crying, and with the cross at her back her words are premonitory: "The world can only be saved through peace, but the whole world will have peace only if it finds God. Reconcile yourselves, be brothers!"

On the fourth day, the six children are summoned to the police office and undergo a very long interrogation that also includes medical-psychiatric examinations. They are announced to be perfectly sane. Once freed, they run to the hill so as to not miss the apparition. Today she talks about priests ("They must be firm in the faith and help you. They must protect the people's faith") and need to believe without the apparitions.

By day five, the crowd had grown to fifteen thousand people. This day, a returning priest questions the six visionaries to evaluate their good faith. At first, I was skeptical, but the words from the six young people are so spontaneous and with no contradictions. He slowly begins to believe them.

On day six, the visionaries are taken to the hospital, and twelve doctors cruelly do another psychiatric examination. The doctors are hoping to establish mental illness but determines the kids are not crazy. That evening, during the apparition, among the crowd is a three-year-old boy seriously ill with septicemia. He is unable to speak or walk. His desperate parents ask for the intercession of Our Lady to heal the boy. She consents but says the entire community and, in particular, the two parents pray, fast, and live on authentic faith. The boy improves every day, and by the end of the summer, he is able to walk and talk. This is the first of over two hundred miracles related to the apparitions occurring, which are going on to this day. The children got older but continue to be tested and are still incredibly sane!

That gives you a short version of an incredible story. In today's world, it seems the nonbelievers outnumber us. They have tried many new technologies to discredit the apparitions, but they are still held real. The popes, over the years, have not fully endorsed the apparitions are real, but they have a hard time discrediting when the millions of people have made the pilgrimage and received the graces and wonderful reinforcements of their faith.

Below is a picture of the hill that we climbed to be where the Blessed Mother continues to appear to the visionaries. It is now called Apparition Hill.

This is the rocky hill where the apparitions take place. It's hard to see from the picture, but it is really a rocky, quite steep, and high long hill. We struggled to get here, but there was no one trying to speed us up. We went at our own pace.

St. James Church built to honor the Blessed Virgin Mary.

The beautiful roses are always associated with Our Lady. As I was leaving Medjugorje, I was smelling roses. The smell continued as I traveled home. It was so strong and ended for me when I was nearing home in North Dakota. I can't explain it, but it was there just like I had cut fresh flowers. I'm assuming Our Lady was traveling with me. Was she protecting me from any trouble? If so, she did a wonderful job and must have figured when I was close to home, I would be okay. Thank you.

The Cross on Krisevac Mountain.

The above picture is the trail on the way to the top of Kristeva Mountain, at Medjugorje in Bosnia and Herzegovina. Mary Beth, Rita, and I made the very long, rocky climb to the top of this mountain to worship. The climb in person is much steeper than the picture shows. It was here while I was climbing that I had my own vision; the visionaries appeared to be actually floating up the hill. It was incredible.

While there, we were invited to stay at the home of one of the visionaries. Her name was Mirjana Dragicevic. We were so blessed to see her home and be allowed to stay with her. She has spent so much time delivering on the requests Our Lady has asked the visionaries to do. I certainly have so much respect for her, and I am not sure I could handle all the questions the visitors ask about the holy site. This trip was so wonderful, and my companions were also overwhelmed.

I have one more thing to report. I traveled with a couple of rosaries of which one was all black in color. I used it to pray on Apparition Hill so knew what it looked like. The reason I say that is because when I returned home, the crucifix had changed from black in color to gold. I literally had to look a few times as I thought maybe my eyes were playing tricks on me. It's real!

I returned again to Medjugorje a few years later. I was traveling again with local church people, but the experience was still the same. I have never felt so much love as I spent time in the presence of Our Lady and the six visionaries, who now have become young adults. They are still called regularly by the Blessed Mother to come and pray the Rosary with her. They receive a message to share with the thousands of followers that are present at any given period. Like I said earlier, the apparitions are continuing today. No other apparitions have stayed this long.

A little update on the disclaimer here for you. Pope Francis and his representatives, along with others in the Catholic Church, have not fully recognized this as a true site that apparitions are happening—yet. Please understand, as you've seen with the beautification of St. Bernadette from Lourdes, this is not a fast process. It takes years of checking all the facts and people, but it is being reported as to be favorable and could happen soon. I have my own proof although I would have believed it anyway because of the feelings I had when present there. I pray my Rosary often that there will be many conversions happening to nonbelievers or, at least, the return to faith of those who left.

Sedona, Arizona

In 2016 I was spending time in Arizona. This was the "Year of Mercy" for the Catholic Church. Mary Beth and Jim were in Arizona also, visiting Kevin and Becky. Since it was the year of mercy, we decided we would do something special to honor Christ. Kevin and Becky had been to a special Catholic chapel in the Sedona, Arizona, area. It sounded like the perfect place to go see, so the five of us left early one morning and made the three-hour drive to visit the chapel. It is built into a rock outcropping.

The Chapel of Mercy is built in the rock.

As I entered through the huge holy glass doors, I could see out the entire south side through the biggest windows. The sky was so beautiful with the puffy cumulus clouds floating by. There were pews inside, some empty, so we sat to pray. I was looking out into the clouds, and it happened so suddenly. I saw Jesus sitting as though he was waiting for me, and then I saw my face come from the clouds, white hair and all. All I could think was what a grace and blessing that was in the "Year of Mercy."

The windows of the Chapel of Mercy.

Jesus has shown me so much mercy as one of his forlorn children I can never praise or thank Him enough. It is really interesting that Mary Beth and Kevin both had visions of their own. It was just such a holy place. Below is a prayer to use to pray the Chaplet of Divine Mercy in honor of the "Year of Mercy."

THE CHAPLET OF THE DIVINE MERCY

(For private recitation on ordinary rosary beads)

Our Father..., Hail Mary..., The Apostles' Creed.

Then, on the OUR FATHER BEADS YOU WILL SAY THE FOLLOWING WORDS:

Eternal Father, I offer You the Body and Blood, Soul and Divinity of Your dearly beloved Son, Our Lord Jesus Christ, in atonement for our sins and those of the whole world.

On the HAIL MARY BEADS you will say the following words:

For the sake of His sorrowful Passion have mercy on us and on the whole world.

In conclusion THREE TIMES you will recite these words:

Holy God, Holy Mighty One, Holy Immortal One, have mercy on us and on the whole world.

(From the Diary of the Servant of God Sr. Faustina Note Book 1, p. 197

IMPRIMATUR: • Joseph F. Maguire
November 17, 1979 Bishop of Springfield, Mass.

It's nice to also pray this during the time of praying the Rosary.

This concludes all the trips I took to worship the Blessed Virgin Mary and our Lord Christ. I have made it my mission since then to be a stronger witness to my faith. There may be some of you that know me personally that may indeed tire of me pushing my Catholic faith. I don't think God tires of helping you when asked, so I've decided I won't tire of doing His work here on earth either. Starting here below, I am going to share some of my own personal reasons to believe in God.

My personal apparitions

When I made my first confession and was saying my penance, I saw a golden Jesus, about eight inches high, go to the altar and tabernacle, and then He was gone. How that stayed with me.

I worked for this one family, and their sister was nun. She was very pretty, and God really had me thinking about my own vocation. There are times it seemed I could have served Him more as a nun, but I'm glad I chose my life even with its challenges.

I was coming home one afternoon with Daddy on a Saturday afternoon and was thinking I had to go to confession. In an instant, I had been given a thought of how eternity went on forever. This scared me to get to confession. I just knew hell was forever.

When I went to Medjugorje, there were so many things that showed God's presence. One was I could look right at the sun and the pretty colored rays around and from the sun. At adoration there was a light in the candle holder that just seemed to go from the top to the bottom on the inside all the while I was there. It happened on both trips—a little hard to describe, but of course, the holder wasn't made with a light.

In the house by the highway, I had a bedroom where I kept all the statues and things of Our Blessed Mother. One night I looked into the room, and all of the air was the prettiest blue color I've ever seen. I knew Mother Mary wanted me to remember her always.

There was one time when we were saying the Rosary once a week with my friends from church. We called it our rosary group. One of those times, I felt Mother Mary's presence right beside me. I just had to look to see if She was still there—gone, but I still felt such a closeness.

Praying for Mom after she died, I wondered if she was in heaven. One night in a dream God, gave me this beautiful yellow rose—it was like Mom and Jesus were there giving it to me. I miss my dear parents so much and wish they were here to share life's ups and downs. I know they aren't forgetting any of us.

I was reading from the Bible one time; Mother Mary's entire profile was among the words. I wish I would have kept it, but I'm sure it was just for me when I needed Her the most.

At adoration of the Eucharist one day, I saw a shadowed face of Jesus in the host. It was a quick flash, but what a feeling I had. Praise God for His loving moments.

One night I was sitting at the head of the bed, and a sin which I had not confessed came to mind. Oh, how I wanted to get to confession right then. This kept me awake most of the night as it was serious enough to make me wonder what would happen if I didn't confess it before death. I got it confessed and forgiven. Praise God for His blessings!

Lastly, I had a heavenly thought. I wanted to erect a large statue of Our Lady or a crucifix on the big hill along Highway

5 at Hank's corner. Rita and I worked on it to the point of finding out it was too expensive. Should have done a little bit at a time.

Throughout the pages here, I have shown my unending love for the Blessed Virgin Mary. Below are a couple of pictures and the statues of her I kept at home. These are in the room that I had the apparition whereby the air in the entire room turned a beautiful blue.

My collection of Our Blessed Mother statues.

As I begin to end the words here in part 3, I want to add just a few prayers and thoughts I've had over the years. My hope has been, in this part of the book, that you truly grasped how my faith in the Lord and the Blessed Mother are so strong. The very first words were I am now and always have been a devout Catholic. I'm so glad to have shared all this with you!

A prayer for you

Love of God and one another is all that matters in this life. All we have done—we give up in the end. What did we do for others and God? He won't question us on wealth or what great things we did in our lifetime. Only what was done in His name and for Him will matter. Would He be proud of us if we did all for Him? What was given us was all from Him. Do we give back to Him for what He has done for you? Remember, all was His for us to use during our lifetime. If He has greatly given to you, give generously back to Him. Love one another too as He has loved you. The greatest love we can ever attain is eternity with Him.

As I go on, children, only one thing matters—the saving of your soul to attain heaven forever. Think of the word *forever*. We want to be with God in heaven forever and please God, not in hell forever. Sin is always with us, and God knows I committed many venial and mortal sins to my disgrace but was able to rid them all through confession. A general confession later in life is so essential. God will forgive these sins, and you will not have to answer for them. It's like He threw them in the ocean and has forgotten them forever. In general confession, we tell all of all the sins of our entire life. The times don't really matter if we don't remember and if we forget some. One has such a relief and a better prospect of death when we meet God. Keeping the slate clean, we must go to regular confession often; and if not done once a year at Easter, we have committed a very grave sin. At night, before we go to sleep, say an act of contrition for all the sins committed that day. How are we prepared to meet God in case He should call us home? May we all enjoy heaven and one another with God.

You were never forgotten in my prayers, my greatest treasure. If you are young, look to God as He will be there for you all your life. If you are older, look back on God's being there for you through all. Whatever your age, know that God's love is the foundation upon which we all live and die for!

As I talk of praying, I will relate the story of a bird outside at the home. It would always start to sing about four o'clock in the morning. It used to upset me until I thought that it was probably praising God with its song. That bird helped me to do a better job of my morning prayers. The point is look at what annoys you and offer it up to God. Also remember to pray daily the act of contrition, and be sure to offer all the days' works to God.

Some random thoughts

I think we are all on the same path, and I think God knew that when He gave us confession. He did this to help us on our way to being in heaven for eternity and maybe even sainthood.

Loving is hard, but for parents, their love is just like the love of Jesus. As He said, there is no greater love than the love for one another. All children have different personalities and ways, but one cannot be loved more than another.

Forgiveness is absolutely necessary to enter heaven when we are called home. Think about this again—does God hem and haw about forgiving your sins in confession? He does not hold back on forgiveness. You may not always forget so easily, but you have to say you are sorry.

Words we say to others have a way of hurting, and lots of times, we don't realize what or how caused our words to hurt. Many times, what we say was never meant to be mean and cause pain to others.

Today I was giving some thought to "mortal sin" (the worst sin because you thought about it before you did it). I am guilty of some of these and wondering if God cancels out all the good deeds you've done up to the point in time when you confess this sin. If it is so, I don't know if I have enough time to make it all up at this late in life. If so, think of all the things that had no value to God up to confessing it. I think I must study a bit more using the Catholic Catechism. I will look it up now!

There are some things in life that are harder than others. For me, there are two heartaches. One is that some of the children have left the Catholic faith. I pray every day, asking God to change hearts. Second is how much the family has been torn apart by what happened to the girls. My true hope is to have some kind of forgiveness for one another. We may not have a chance for the last rites and the apostolic blessing before we die. We will have to face God at death's instantly, and may God help us all to be ready to meet Him.

I made a trip to Leroy Church lately. I went to pray and gain what is called a plenary indulgence. This is a great way to have all your sins forgiven and load up on God's graces. This can be made in the "Year of Faith" by praying at the church you were baptized in and made your first Communion. Then go to confession and receive Holy Communion within eight days.

I would like to especially thank God for all His blessings bestowed on me which have helped me give all to Him. No worries, just prayers and thanksgiving. I am so glad to be able to enjoy my days here at the home. I have some pains and problems, but when I look around, it could be much worse for me. I pray for God to grant me a "happy death," and again, nothing else matters but to be with Jesus forever and ever.

This ends part 3. Part 4 is next and will be full of fun and an upbeat atmosphere. Enjoy.

Part 4

Who Is Doreen Dettler? Fifty-One Story-Worth Questions

Who is Cecilia Doreen Dettler? The following pages contain some fun, emotional, and crazy questions and answers. They are arranged in no particular order. Some of the answers are long, and some are short for no reason either. Enjoy!

1. What are a few of your favorite memories?

    a. When Grandma Koropatnicki told me I won a car and then brought it to me at home, I couldn't believe it. I had bought a $1 chance to win a car at the Walhalla Catholic Church. They were selling the chances on a new 1949 Chevrolet custom sedan. One ticket is all it took. Thinking back now, I don't remember ever winning anything of some value again!

A picture of my car again.

Since I was only sixteen and couldn't drive, Daddy suggested I sell it. I sold it for $1,600, and Daddy was my banker. He would give money to me if I could prove that it was going to buy something useful. I guess I learned at an early age the conservativeness of bankers. I remember a few things I bought with money—some kitchen appliances for Mom. The last thing I remember was a new stove for our house after I was married.

b. I mentioned going shopping for a wedding ring earlier. This is still one of my favorite memories. I had my choice of three different ones. I never did know the cost but felt assured that he could afford the one I picked.

c. In school, one of my teachers gave me a book. *Greatest Story Ever Told* was the title, and it enlightened my mind more about God. It seemed to be an extension of the truths I had received after going to Catechism in the summer.

2. What were you like as a teenager?

Not really bad, as I recall. I never went to jail, which was a big blessing. I'm not sure why I even thought about jail here as during the time I'm growing up, jail was such a remote occurrence. I didn't know anyone who went to jail—a bit different than today. Didn't have a lot of parties to do drinking. The first drink of liquor I ever had was on New Year's Eve, before I was married. Aelred and I went to a bar in Walhalla, only had one drink, and don't even remember what it was. I knew at that point that alcohol wasn't for me! I recall one memory here about the only time I got disciplined by Mom. During the winter on the farm, water near the wood stove would be available to wash up in the morning as the stove would keep the ice blocks melted during the night. Anyway, Mom asked me to go wash up before we left for Mass on Sunday morning. I told her I had done it already, but Rita came and told Mom the water was frozen, so there was no way I could have washed. I got a licking for that, and it was the only time I ever told Mom a lie. I felt horrible for what I had said and really don't know why I did it!

3. What did you find surprising when you started your first job?

My first job away from the farm was a waitress at a café in Cavalier. This was after my freshman and sophomore years of high school. The tips were a big surprise, but I worked with an older lady, and she seemed to be quite jealous of the tips I got. Thank God when I won the car, I quit the serving job.

4. Did you move as a child? What was the experience like?

I was always excited especially after we moved to the Swanson farm. Wasn't so thrilled when we moved to the other places. The Swanson house was big enough for me to have my own room. Also we had a clothes closet but still never had a bathroom, so there is no toilet or running water but still had the outhouse!

5. Have you ever wished to be a celebrity or famous for something?

Never! Nothing!

6. Did you get along with your siblings as a child?

Yes, and possibly they liked me because I could and would take care of them.

7. Are you a morning person or an evening person?

I am a morning person—early to bed and early to rise! As my children were growing up, I liked to get them to bed around eight, then I would have some time for myself to get things done. This really was a double-edged sword for me. Let me explain. Yes, they were in bed early, but now they would be up by 5:30 a.m. I would have worked late on my projects, and they were always the early risers, so for a period of time while they were growing up, I guess I would have been an evening person, but today, as I reside in the home, I'm always up early.

8. What is your best advice for raising children?

Tell them how it should be, and stick to your words. If it is mealtime or snack time, be at the table. Do not wander around the house with food. This is just easier for moms as the cleaning up is easier.

Today the schools are doing the sex education and doing it way too early. Personally, I think this should be the parents' job and as parents we will know when it's time for the "talk." I always felt, I suppose, give it my all!

9. What are your favorite possessions? Why?

My family and holy spiritual pictures, the many rosaries I've collected over the years from the trips I've taken, and sick-call crucifix. All these have led me through the good and bad times as only God can do.

10. How has your life turned out differently than you imagined as a teenager?

I suppose, like most teenagers, I never gave much thought to life back then. Lived and went from one day to the next. As you have read in the earlier parts of the book, I have been satisfied with my life except for a few things.

11. Have you been the recipient of a random act of kindness?

I have experienced many, many acts of kindness. I hope I've been thankful enough for all these. I do hope everyone knows that even if I never said thank you, it was in my heart, and I say it now.

12. What is the best meal you ever had?

Lots and lots of good ones, but without a doubt, the very best meals were the ones at Grandma Koropatnicki's house. It was just hard to beat Ukrainian cooking at Christmas and Easter. Grandma went all out cooking perogies (potatoes, cheese, and meat rolled in dough and boiled or fried) and holopsi—these were meat rolled in cabbage and cooked with rice). Mom never made these as Dad was a meat-and-potatoes kind of guy. She never wanted to upset the "apple cart."

13. Who are your all-time favorite musicians or bands?

I have always been a lover of country music. My favorite was Hank Williams. Next favorite would have been Charlie Pride. Before we were married, Aelred asked me if I really liked that kind of music. I said I did and always felt he really liked music with an Irish flair. I suppose since Grandma Bea (his mother) was 100 percent Irish, she liked Irish songs, and it was passed to him.

14. What were your favorite subjects in high school?

My favorite was home economics. I had a hard time in school but eventually got through high school. I did also like English class. After starting my freshman year, I brought home algebra homework and asked Dad to help me with it. All he said was "What in the hell is that" so he was no help as he had only gone to the fourth grade. He was tremendous with math when it came to dollars though!

15. Where did you go on vacation as a child?

I never went anywhere. My parents never went anywhere either. Our trips were confined to visiting our relatives. This was very common when I grew up. Most families were not spread out across county or state borders. Thus, it was easier to spend time with them and much cheaper.

16. What is one of the stupidest things you've ever done?

As I think back, there was a time when we bought a new car, and it really wasn't needed. We did enjoy new cars even if they were a poor investment.

17. What were your grandparents like?

Dad's parents: I only saw his father a few times. It was only when I would tag along as Daddy went to shave or cut his hair. Grandpa died young, and I only remember him being in bed. Grandma Carignan lived with us during the winters as her house was a cold shack. Thus, I got to know her. She was good to us, but we knew we had to be good. She didn't have any patience for misbehaving.

Mom's parents: Her parents were Ukrainian, so it was hard to get to know them because their English was not great. Grandpa Koropatnicki was very quiet and gentle. Grandma was a hard worker. An example here, she was out stacking hay just three days after having a newborn at the house. We liked her because she always let us eat rhubarb with salt.

18. What fascinated you as a child?

During the summer months, I was able to stay in Leroy with my Grandma Carignan. I went to Mass every morning with her. I was eight years old, and I was so thrilled to be able to do this. I also enjoyed the beautiful purple petunias that Grandma grew. Their smell was so wonderful. It's odd that the same flowers today don't have the great smell. Grandma's simple way of life was something I wish I could have inherited from her.

19. What was one of the strangest things you wanted when you were growing up?

I hated wearing long johns under a dress all the time. I was so glad when those went away, but I didn't gain much as the stockings replaced the long johns, and now we needed to wear garters to hold up the long socks. Didn't really gain that much.

20. What would you save if your house was on fire?

My family pictures.

21. What advice would you give your great grandchildren?

I would try to instill in them the absolute importance that God needs to be number one in their lives. Also never doubt your faith as without Him, the journey of life with be so hard. With Him, anything can be tackled and made well.

22. What gift did you always wish someone would give you?

My wish is always the same. I want to receive the gift of love during the Christmas season. I always wanted a beautiful lamp that Rita had. She said no problem and was going to give it to me when I went to visit her. It never happened. I did get my wish as Rita left it to me when she died a few years ago.

23. What are some favorite memories of each of your children when they were growing up?

Kevin: so good in school, very smart, so young.

Mary Beth: Always a real help to me. Never hesitated to get something for me when needed.

Steven: A good baby. I never gave him much attention. He was so good.

Chalmer: His love of books. Very good at sports, especially wrestling. Loved his easygoing nature.

David: Wasn't any trouble. Was always good at home.

Joni: So happy to have another daughter. Was also easy to take care of.

Don't know why there weren't more children, but it was God's plan, and we lived in His way.

24. What early memories do you have of your siblings?

I was home only until the boys were growing up. Rita was married, so I was with the boys more. The best story I remember about the boys happened about a visit from Aelred. He had showed up at the farm to ask me to go to the show with him. It had rained a good amount, and he got stuck with his car in the "gumbo" soil. He was wearing his shiny shoes, and they were full of the "gumbo soil." The boys laughed so hard, and I know they never forgot that.

25. Have you ever doubted your faith?

No! Never, never ever!

26. How has the country changed in your lifetime?

It is going to hell a bit every day! There is such a great divide between the Republicans and Democrats that wasn't so pronounced years ago. As a conservative, I find it so hard to understand what the Democrats are doing. They believe you can kill babies even after they are born. Allowing people to vote without any ID and allowing young children to have operations without the parents' consent is so unbelievable—and let's not forget the open border and we now have our $34,000,000,000,000 debt. How can our country continue to exist?

27. Are you more like your father or mother?

I think more like my Dad; he never seemed to be on the outs with anyone. I wish I had inherited his frugal use of money. I'm not saying I'm terrible with the spending, just not as good as Daddy. My faith in God came from mother. As you've read already, my faith was also bolstered by Grandma Fritz. I remember her going to the crucifix and standing, beating her breast and praying in Ukrainian. She truly always relied on Him.

28. What foods do you dislike? Have these changed over time?

I have never had a real dislike for any particular food or ingredients. That hasn't changed over the years.

29. How did you decide to get married?

I dated a man in the last year of high school. I thought he was the "number one." Then after graduating, I meant to work for Sid and Charlotte Chaput. They lived about six miles southwest of Langdon. The Dettler farm was only a quarter mile south of the Chaputs. Aelred was a regular visitor at the Chaputs, and I met him there. I knew immediately that if I ever had a chance to see him again, there would be no way I could marry the man I was dating. God heard my prayers and I did see Aelred again and love flourished. There are so many times you hear of "love at first sight"—certainly was true in my case.

30. Tell about one of your best days ever?

The day here contains both the saddest and the best together. Aelred revealed to me the things he had done to Mary Beth and at the same time apologized to her. This wouldn't seem to qualify as one of the best, but it was, as Mary Beth forgave his sins. As a true Catholic, forgiveness is such a huge part of our beliefs that I was saddened but then elated. Enough said.

31. Who has been one of the most important people in your life? Tell about him or her.

I have been blessed my entire life to have had so many friends and relatives that were extremely important, but lately I am going to give credit to Father Metzger, who was helping at St. Alphonsus in Langdon. I asked if he would come to hear my confession. He did, and with him I was able to make a "general confession." All the sins of my past life that I could remember and those I may have forgotten were forgiven at that moment. I wished God would have called me home right then. I had received the greatest gift from confession. God will never remember the sins you have confessed nor will He punish you for them—great consolation as there will be no purgatory for those sins. This is available for all that practice the Catholic faith.

32. How is life different today compared to when you were a child?

It seems most people have plenty of money. My parents appeared to only have enough for a small livelihood. Many, many people are doing so well financially—nice houses (with electricity and running water, LOL), new cars, some lake homes, some mountain homes, and money put away for retirement. When I was growing up, most of our relatives lived within a few miles of us. Now it takes a fair amount of money just to go visit relatives as they live across the country or even overseas.

33. Do you have any moving-day stories?

Not really, but I'll bet my brothers and sisters thought we would never settle down. The entire family was so much help even at young ages. Then, like times of babies being born, there were always the relatives around, and they helped on moving day.

34. What place or places would you like to travel to over and over?

Kevin and Becky's home in Arizona. I made trips to Medjugorje and Lourdes and would love to return. I wish I could have gone to Wisconsin where the Blessed Mother appeared, also a trip to Mexico to see "Our Lady of Guadalupe." There are so many sacred places that should be on a Catholic's bucket list: Rome, the Vatican, and Bethlehem. Do it before getting a little older holds you back.

35. What was one of the greatest physical challenges you ever had to go through? What gave you strength?

I hurt my back, which was the reason for going to the care home. My strength was faith that Almighty God would care for me if I put my faith in Him, and so He has, and I am so happy now with my life.

36. How did you celebrate your thirtieth birthday?

I was with the children. Kevin was eleven and the rest smaller. It was summer, and with no school, they could wear me down during those eighteen hours of daylight we have on June 21. There was no money for celebrating. Grandma Bea made me a cake, and I'm sure the children enjoyed as did I.

37. Do you believe people can change? Why?

I really don't know. Things today are so different, and many people are headed in the wrong direction with their lives. It seems that people have things very good today, and some have abandoned their faith and prayers. God can get us to where we should be, but most will only turn back to Him when things begin to go poorly. I guess at that point, they should change. I guess in this scenario people can change.

38. Did you ever have a fair or carnival come to town when you were a child?

No carnivals came to town, but we were allowed to go to the Pembina county fair and the Hamilton fair. Growing up, there were many more fairs than today. People didn't want to travel very far to attend. Money was an issue, and reliable transportation also an issue, but more of the population attended. How we looked forward to the fair days. After I was older, I babysat on Saturday night, then Mom and Daddy went that night.

On a side note, I remember one day that Santa Claus came to the show hall in Cavalier, he gave us a paper bag of peanuts and a few candies. This was a big deal, much like the food we got at the fair. Of course, to see Santa was really something!

39. As a child, were you closer to your father or mother?

I was closer to my mom. I think most things I learned came from her. Dad was not in the house much because of all the outdoor things that needed to be done—for instance, cattle and crop production. The boys probably learned most things from Dad as they were always working on farm things too, but they spent some time with Mom so certainly gained some knowledge there.

40. What did you wear as a teenager that mortifies you today?

I don't recall anything, but I wore a nice dress which I bought myself using babysitting money. It cost $8. I ordered it through a catalog, probably Sears. I wore long stockings and don't think I ever wore a pair that didn't end up with a run in them. This would be grounds for mortifying today, but then Mom didn't buy very many stockings, so they were worn at times with runs!

41. How far back can you trace your family history?

I have only gone back to my parents. They came from the "old country." Back then we did not have the internet to find out about them like we do nowadays. When I was young, the information we received about our ancestry came from word of mouth when visiting our grandparents or other relatives. I think that now there are others that have investigated more of our history.

42. What did you hide from your parents as a child?

I do not remember anything. There may have been times I hid things from the younger ones in the family like Santa, Easter bunny, or tooth fairy. I do not think I was ever a deceitful person.

43. What things do you think you cannot live without?

Now at my age, I need a wristwatch to use if I am in trouble, like falling. These should be on any older person. For sure a medical alert device. This was so great when I fell and broke my hip. Without it, I would have laid there for hours before someone could have found me.

44. Which Easter traditions are most important to you?

The Easter Masses, Holy Thursday, Good Friday, Holy Saturday, and of course, Easter Sunday Mass. When I was a child, we gave up eating between meals, but sometimes Mom would give us a slice of fresh baked bread. When the afternoon of Holy Saturday came, we did not have to do that anymore. Back to normal! The Easter season is the most important time of year for me as there are many of our Catholic beliefs happening then.

45. How did you vote in the last election?

Always Republican.

46. What advice do you wish you had taken from your parents?

I can't recall anything, but I do know they always said to be good when left for a date—and I was!

47. How did you rebel as a child?

I did not. I knew what the consequences would be, and I did not want that to happen—a good spanking! Today kids can have their phones taken away, internet surfing time reduced, or even loss of their cars instead of spankings. Which method of parenting is better, I do not know, but I do know that in my young life, the idea of a spanking kept me out of trouble. I reality, you learned earlier in the book of the one and only spanking I received from my mother for lying. I never did get a spanking from Daddy.

48. What TV programs did you watch as a child?

TV, what was that? We did not have a TV until after I was married and had three children. Even then, it would be hard to call it TV. It was mostly a box with a screen with a lot of snowylike interference and voices that could be described as muffled. But as years went by, the quality continued, to this day, to get better. As the children got older, it was really hard to keep them from wanting to watch. They were just fascinated with it. They would sneak out of their upstairs rooms at night, lie up on the stairs to watch the TV in the living room. There was only one TV for the entire house instead of eleven in some homes! Kevin, I'm picking on you for fun.

49. What was your neighborhood like when you were growing up?

As you know, we lived on a farm. Back then there were many more farms scattered across the countryside than today. Most farmers had a little cropland and enough pasture to raise a few cattle. There might be a farm every one-quarter to one-half mile. Today farms might occur one every five miles or more. This is the reason for the country schools back then. That kept the walking distance as it was the usual means of travel. I know you hear the stories of how we walked to and from school for five miles each way and uphill both ways. Well, that is exaggerated, but we did walk to school as you read earlier.

So the neighborhood could be described as quiet, and at night, you could add that it was dark also as there were very few farms with electricity, thus no yard lights. Of course, no phones, and our parents rarely went out at night, so only conversation kept us occupied. Using only oil lamps to light the interior of our house meant we went to bed early, and were always up and going at dawn.

50. What was your big trip?

As you read in part 2, my first big trip was our honeymoon. Growing up, there simply was not money to be going much, but this trip was incredible. At the risk of repetition, I'm going to repeat parts of it.

We left January 21,1953, for Dayton, Ohio. Aelred's sister Moira lived there. Her husband, Vince, was in the Air Force at Wright-Patterson Air Base. It took three days to get there, and I was so thrilled to see all the new country. We had such a fun time touring the air base and visiting. I always enjoyed Moria as she seemed to be so educated. They had a couple of boys, Jerry and Terry, when we were there. They went on to have three more children.

The scenery heading to Michigan was very exciting and may be because I had never seen anything like it back home. The next part of the journey took us to Indianna to the cousins of Aelred. The Deiners were very successful farmers and businessmen, and it showed. Their farms were very nice. The soil was so black, and farming was so important that they farmed every acre they could. They remained lifelong friends as we went to visit them more than once, always stayed in touch with Christmas cards and letters.

51. What is the longest project you ever worked on?

The answer is really two projects. One was the little doll or clown clothes we made for the air purifiers (Air Wick). We did these for a lot of years. Second, though, has to be making donuts and baked goods. This went on for at least twenty-eight years. That was a long time, but it didn't seem that bad. Certainly kept us busy!

Printed in the USA
CPSIA information can be obtained
at www.ICGtesting.com
CBHW071622150824
13132CB00038B/507